Poet, performer, educator, Mark
Bruford College in Theatre. Retr
Goldsmiths College in 2004. He
performing his poetry and facilit
identity and poetics.

Publishing *Mixed Messages* in 2009, he has toured nationally,
taking his poems as far afield as Johannesburg in person and
worldwide online from Ronnie Scott's to the Paralympics.

Featured on Radio 4, BBC Radio London, Jazz FM and Choice
FM, his commissions include work with The Royal Maritime
Museum, the charities The ACLT and Crisis, as well as BBC Radio
Four, for whom he crafted a suite of poems for 'Lights Out: From
the Ashes of New Cross' in 2020.

A founder of the 'Poetry in London' Facebook group, Thompson
has curated and hosted events from 'Lipped Ink' at the
Poetry Society Café, to 'Fighting Talk' at Greenwich Theatre
and monthly online events 'Poetry from the Grassroots'.

In print he has featured in the Morning Star and three anthologies
since 2020; *Poets Against Trump*, *Football is Poetry* and
Poetry is our Protest - a collaboration with Spoken with whom
he also contributed to a poetry exchange with Born Lippy in
Newcastle in 2021.

Mark hosted local Black Lives Matter events in 2020 and
contributed poetry to commemorations of 'The Battle of
Lewisham' and the New Cross fire, helping to immortalise local
moments in Black British history.

With a children's picture book in development, poetry workshops
for East Side Educational Trust and contributing to a transatlantic
webinar with Digital Theatre+ on the history of Black poetry in
English, there's been a lot going on!

'Philosophers can keep interpreting the world, it's us who needs
to change it!'

More Mixed Messages

Mark 'Mr T' Thompson

Burning Eye

BurningEyeBooks
Never Knowingly
Mainstream

Copyright © 2022 Mark 'Mr T' Thompson
Cover design by Catherine Whiteoak

This edition published by Burning Eye Books 2022

www.burningeye.co.uk

@burningeyebooks

Burning Eye Books
15 West Hill, Portishead, BS20 6LG

ISBN 978-1-913958-34-3

Today I didn't change the world,
at least not very much.
I did not win a lottery,
nor save some other's life.
But on my way
I tried to help the few that I did touch,
by finding hope in poetry
when hopelessness was rife.

CONTENTS

MESSAGES ON...
THE PANDEMIC AND BEING WELL

MESSAGES ON...
POLICY, POLITICS AND PEOPLE

MESSAGES ON...
WORK AND PLAY

INTRODUCTION

As an artist, an educator, a performer and an activist, I'm always trying to effect change. Sometimes just by the retelling of tales at risk of being forgotten, but often by holding up a mirror to the world, with a reflection familiar and yet distorted enough to help myself and others understand and challenge where we are.

Putting together a retrospective collection of my own poetry has been a curious process. This is particularly true because, as a jobbing spoken word artist, I have written a lot of poems over the dozen years or so since I wrote *Mixed Messages*, many of them for very specific audiences, events or commissions. Unsurprisingly, this has led to a disparate and eclectic output of words: some written to order, some written with purpose, some written to recount stories or express emotions that I needed to capture somewhere for the sake of preserving my limited sanity.

Some of these words are clearly not obvious bedfellows. However, they represent moments of a personal journey through the last decade and my desire to document and better understand myself, my heritage, the way our world works and how, all too often, it unfortunately appears that it doesn't.

I have split the pieces into five broad categories, and have given each chapter a preface.

www.marktpoetry.com

MESSAGES ON... RACE

'Intolerants Not Welcome' was indirectly commissioned for a series of events organised by Goldsmiths University to mark the fortieth anniversary of the infamous Battle of Lewisham. Anti-racists clashed with the fascists of the National Front, whose march from New Cross was never allowed to reach its final destination in the heart of Lewisham. The poem was recorded live at the unveiling of a plaque on Clifton Rise and broadcast on BBC Radio 4, and was selected for Radio 4's Pick of the Week. Open Eye Film also produced a short, which was screened at the BFI as part of SOUL Celebrate:Connect.

'New Cross' was first read prior to the unveiling of a blue plaque to mark the site of the New Cross fire of 1977. The suite of poems 'From the Ashes of New Cross' was commissioned to be a narrative spine for a Radio 4 documentary about the same events, which aired in 2020. The documentary, the Lights Out episode 'From the Ashes of New Cross', was nominated for both an ARIA and an Amnesty International Media Award.

'My Ends' is a response to the number of high-rise buildings that have been thrown up in Lewisham over the last decade, within a few minutes' walk of where I've lived since I was a kid. I stretched the piece to also explore the concept of dementia, which both my grandmothers experienced at the end of their lives. One of the first signs of the illness in my paternal grandma was that she completely forgot who I was. This piece was first published in a special edition of the magazine Token as part of the Deptford Literature Festival 2022, funded by Lewisham Borough of Culture. The first reading was filmed at Mind Over Matter Brixton and shared on social media.

'One of Us' was written to mark the twentieth anniversary of the racist murder of Stephen Lawrence, near Eltham in the borough of Greenwich.

'Stay Put' is a response to the terrible fire in the Grenfell tower. It focuses on the principle 'stay put', a fire policy that has been in place since the 1960s and which I first became aware of when I lived on the top floor of a tower block in Newcastle in 1992. This policy, alongside poor maintenance and the retrofitted cladding, was considered to be a significant factor in the seventy-two deaths in the fire. The poem, like the tower, is twenty-four lines tall.

'He Saw a Hooded Figure' came to me on the morning after the Zimmerman trial, following the murder of Trayvon Martin, while I was contemplating the gunman's acquittal. This death and the associated miscarriage of justice would be the spark that led to the initial explosion of the Black Lives Matter campaign.

'If You Don't Understand Us' has been adapted, with the name of the young person changed in performance to that of the latest death of a black man after police contact. It was initially a response to the deaths of Rashan Charles and Edson Da Costa in East London in 2017.

'We Didn't Wanna Watch' was a response to the film showing the murder of George Floyd by police in the US city of Minneapolis, which reignited the Black Lives Matter campaign worldwide in 2020. It was first read at a number of socially distanced BLM events in South London, and was subsequently made into a short film by Muddy Feet Poetry in 2021.

'Only Criminal If' draws parallels between looting during protests that followed the death of George Floyd and the historic pillaging of artefacts by Europeans, highlighting the blinkered hypocrisy of the media reactions at the time. Examples could have included items from the sacking of Benin City to the pyramids, but I chose the Parthenon Marbles. These are better known here as the Elgin Marbles, after Lord Elgin, who effectively looted them from Athens whilst the Greeks were under the rule of the Ottoman empire. This poem was broadcast on the BBC Radio 4 podcast Short Cuts.

'Seed of the Fruit' was commissioned by the National Maritime Museum Greenwich to mark the United Nations International Day for the Remembrance of the Slave Trade and its Abolition.

It was subsequently re-recorded, ankle-deep in the mud on the banks of the River Thames at Greenwich, and broadcast on BBC Radio 4.

'Dis Place' was commissioned for Displaced Histories, a migration-themed poetry event at the Exchange in Ilford.

'The Scratchers and the Scrawlers' started off as one line that fell out of my mouth as I walked away from the New Cross fire plaque unveiling. I went on to use the line 'we shall not forget', which was borrowed from Benjamin Zephaniah's response to the fire, '13 Dead'. An earlier version of this piece was first read on Words Manifest, a poetry feature on Chris Philips' Choice FM show, and subsequently made into a film by Muddy Feet Poetry.

'The Freshest' was commissioned for a set of workshops at the school that was built on the same site as my secondary school, dealing with a concern raised about black pupils referring to each other as FOBs (Fresh Off the Boat) as an insult.

'Reppin fi di lan' plays on a little knowledge of Jamaica to highlight the ignorance of some who might argue having only one Jamaican parent might make me less or even not Jamaican. 'Xaymaca' is the original Taino word for Jamaica and means 'land of wood and water'. Ironwood or lignum vitae, ackee and 'Out of many, one people', are the national flower/wood, fruit and motto of the island.

'Bolt' is barely ten lines long, and can be performed with a swagger in about 9.5 seconds, if you train hard and get a good start. Try it!

The rest of this section is all poems about iconic people from Black History, many of whom have their names in the poem and need no introduction. 'Just Mad Enough' to dream was MLK. Maya Angelou is for me 'The Definition of Phenomenal'. John Carlos and Tommie Smith were banned from athletic competition for 'A Raised Fist' in Mexico in 1968.

'John Blanke' is the first black Briton of record, a trumpeter who appears in the court roll of King Henry VIII in 1511. This poem was commissioned as part of the John Blanke Project to raise awareness of John Blanke's existence through artistic responses to his story and the image of the Tudor trumpeter in the 1511 Westminster Tournament Roll from the College of Arms Collection. Thanks to Ebun Culwin for permission to reproduce her 2018 work *John Blanke Re-Imagined.*

Saint Maurice (AKA Saint Moritz) is a legendary black Roman legionnaire from Thebes in Egypt. Walter Tull was an early black professional footballer and the first British-born black officer in the army when he was commissioned in 1917.

INTOLERANTS NOT WELCOME

An anti-muggers march,
called by mugs who wanted to spread hate,
August thirteenth in seventy-seven:
history demands we mark the date
when south-east London screamed out
for black and white to unite and fight,
ensuring none of these wrong 'uns on the right
would ever again be so bold or bright.

The backward Front was in
for one hell of a surprise;
they'd find Clifton was a hill
up which they just couldn't rise.
So, behind brown-boy-hunting boys in blue
and baton-wielding horsemen,
on Achilles, this most dishonourable guard
wheeled to come again!

But the locals stood firm,
even with kids in our front ranks,
so today, us youngsters
need to give it up and show some thanks
to those old boys and girls
who got up, stood up, and who never come fi play –
the beating heart of Lewisham
who pogo-skanked to block the way.

Some will tell you that we rioted...
and they're not entirely wrong,
but we would not be quieted,
we faced up proud and strong,
landing one thump
'pon fascism's glass chin.
Sure, we fought with the law,
but the law couldn't win,

because these are our streets
and this is our home
where from the cradle
we're rocked by our beats
and mock racists,
who still fear on these roads to roam.

See, what happened on this day is,
as one, our people made it clear –
intolerants, listen up,
unnu are not welcome here!

NEW CROSS

The skyline's changed, but, you know, I wonder
how much has changed for those living under
SE14's ash-grey January shrouds,
which once were swelled by a black plume as charred as hate
and darkened further still by a police response
inappropriate and late.

It was supposed to be a night of great celebration,
not one to create a date of shame for a city and a nation.
Fourteen passed over, many felt as the result of one bigot's action.
Thirty years have passed since; seems we will get no satisfaction
or justice for the potential that was stolen by fire
on a cold winter's night.
Let's hope any perpetrator is not hidden from karma's ire
and all-seeing light.

You may ask, 'What was the reaction from the voices of the establishment?'
Well, with indifferent apathy, 'our government'
let it pass without acknowledgement.
Despite the size of this tragedy,
we saw no messages of goodwill or sympathy,
let alone a visit from a significant dignitary.

But, although with Babylon's old bill
many 'round here were still so obviously angry,
despite the headlines to the contrary,
twenty thousand plus of us went up and demonstrated peacefully.
Those fourteen who died galvanised a community – together.
Although scars even now are carried inside,
memories of this, and you too, will also last forever.

Sure, the skyline has changed, but, you know, I do wonder
just how much has changed for those living under
SE14's stone-grey January shrouds,
which were once swelled by a black plume as charred as hate
and darkened further still by a police response
as inappropriate as it was late.

FROM THE ASHES OF NEW CROSS

Commissioned for Lights Out, BBC Radio 4

1. Fear

Before the first spark
or shard of broken glass
it was here.

Its odour imperceptible,
masked by the sweet treats
and seasoned meats
prepared to feed the throng.
But even before the very first song,
as furniture was moved aside
to clear the floor for feet to fly,
it was here.

And, as the revellers arrived,
if you'd have looked deep
into those pairs of bright young eyes,
or seen the scene when their backsides
were all first moved to move to the beat
in time perhaps against flock walls,
you would be forgiven for struggling to see it.
But still, in a heightened awareness of the exits
for which they'd later have to hurry,
it was here.

And when the music played,
over the thumping bass
it was almost inaudible,
like the fine scratches
in much-loved ancient vinyl
that you try so hard not to hear...
but what is quite clear
is it could be heard.
'Cos it was here.

And it… it was fear.
And it's still here.

2. I see three

They just want to protect us.
Well, that is what they claim.
Just following intelligence.
Well, that's what they choose to blame
when they say we look suspicious.
But then, to some, we all look the same.
So, when they go hunting for one of us,
for all of us, being black becomes a dangerous game.

The police in the US were in fact set up
to catch slaves who ran away,
but it can be dangerous still
for blacks to run… or even walk today.
And while it's true the Brits' boys in blue
don't have that history,
they are often unwelcome and untrusted
by those who look a bit like me.
Because when it's IC3 they hear,
some go blind and get annoyed.
Trigger fingers get itchier, I fear.
Tasers and choke-holds are clearly self-deployed,
since, despite all that Macpherson said,
chiefs argue this institution is no longer racist.
So should we forget those who needlessly ended up dead?
Can our complaints about police failing us now be
dismissed?

3. London

We have seen London burning for all too many years,
and because of fire London has shed all too many tears.
Londoners lost their lives.

Londoners lost their homes.
Londoners' past complaints were just compiled
into old and dusty tomes.
But London won't be ignored.
No, Londoners won't be silenced.
And, although Londoners' protests have been dismissed
as simple-minded violence,
we will still stand up
and we will still speak out
and we will demand justice.
Of that there is no doubt.

4. Whoever

Imagine that your child
was one of the fourteen.
Imagine what you might have thought
after all that you'd seen.

Something must be done.
Something must be said.
Someone must stand up
before some other child lies dead.

None should choke upon the smoke
or should feel the fire's kiss.
No one should be burying their offspring,
ripped from the world like this.

Left with little more than memories
of the lives they barely got to live,
tell me: how could you hope to cope,
let alone ever hope to forgive

whoever was responsible,
whoever lit the fuse?
Who can explain why those in power
remained unmoved by those horrific views

of a home reduced to charcoal
and families drowning in tears,
a community in agony
with such justifiable fears?

So tell them that this wasn't ignited by racism,
and they'll tell you, you might be right.
But few can believe the country's reaction would've been the same
if those kids who died were white.

MY ENDS

I don't recognise my ends no more.
I think I'm near home, but I'm not quite sure.
That looks like the school where I used to go,
but the name has changed, so I just don't know.

I don't recognise my ends no more.
So many new buildings, with so many floors.
Towering above, they make my head spin.
I just wanna go home, but don't know where to begin.

I don't recognise my ends no more.
But the hoorays and hipsters, they weren't here before.
Converting their loft, extending into their basement,
but how do we measure the impact of cultural displacement?

I don't recognise my ends no more.
It seems like there's a near-constant war
for control of the air, the streets, the turf.
Who can calculate what a community's skyline is worth?

I don't recognise my ends no more.
It's got so I'm scared to open my door.
It's hard to admit how much I've forgot,
but trust me when I say it must be a lot.

'Cos I don't recognise my ends no more,
and I can't bear the confusion that I now endure.
Some call me mad, doc says it's dementia.
Now a trip to the corner shop is like a flippin' adventure.

No, I don't recognise my ends no more,
nor that stranger stood there that I used to adore.
He claims that he is the son of my son.
I humour him, and his visit's soon done.

And I don't recognise my ends no more.
I think I'm near home, but I'm not quite sure.
That looks like the school where I used to go,
but the name has changed, so I just don't know.

I don't recognise my ends no more.
So many new buildings, with so many flaws.
Towering above, they make my head spin.
I just wanna go home… I just wanna go home…
I just wanna go home, but don't know where to begin.

STAY PUT

I have a fear of fire.
I have a fear of height.
I have a fear of being trapped alone
on my life's very last night.

I have a fear of towers.
I fear the way they sway,
the way the wind's wicked whispers
whistle past with far too much to say.

I fear some in high places.
I fear they do not care.
I fear they lack compassion.
I can smell it in the air.

I fear some have been greedy.
I fear corners have been cut.
I fear eyes that should be open now
by weight of coin have been shut.

I fear I'd have known the policy;
I fear it 'cos it's true.
I fear my undoing would have been
to do what I'd been told to do.

I fear that I'd still be there
beneath the charcoal-blackened soot.
Yes, I fear that I'd still be there now
because I would've stayed put.

ONE OF US

Stephen Lawrence, 13 September 1974 to 22 April 1993

Twenty years ago, he is waiting for a bus,
'cos twenty years ago, he is simply one of us.
But just twenty years ago, he comes under attack,
just 'cos twenty years ago, this teenager is black.

Twenty years ago, he runs for his life,
'cos twenty years ago, racists stick him with a knife.
Twenty years ago, this firework is far too fleeting,
and so twenty years ago, his brave heart, it will stop beating.

But twenty years ago, when the officers arrive;
yes, just twenty years ago, this young man is still alive!
But twenty years ago, no compassion is displayed,
when, twenty years ago, none will administer first aid.

Twenty years ago, justice is not expected.
Twenty years ago, perpetrators are protected,
as, twenty years ago, the system is unfair
and, twenty years ago, it seems too many do not care.

Twenty years ago, we were right to doubt those wearing blue,
and, though this was twenty years ago, to this day, many still do.

So twenty years have passed since he came under attack.
Yes, twenty years have passed since he was killed for being black.
Twenty years have passed since he waited for a bus,
and twenty years have passed since he was simply one of us.

AGAIN

Mark Duggan, 15 September 1981 to 4 August 2011

A young man
by the law is shot,
unarmed.

Again.

Only twenty feet away, a weapon was supposed to lie,
but, with one 20/20 eye glued on what is not there,
strange CO19 won't miss the flesh that fills their sights.

Again.

After shot one, they spot one
illusive barrel pointed straight at them,
so… fatally… they fire.

Again.

'Gangster in police shootout,'
to the media
they fictionalise.

Again.

'There was another shot…'
or just two,
fired by 'our boys' in blue.

Again.

The order of events
around the scene
has to be changed.

Again

Outside a court,
a mother cries for justice
and in grief.

Again.

But none are caught,
because, of course,
none are to be charged.

Again.

So, justice will not come.
Again.
The elders call for peace.
Again.
We've heard it all before, but still it hurts.

Again.
And again.
And again.

That when a young man,
by the law,
is shot unarmed...

Again.

Guess what.
No shocks.
He's black.

Again.

HE SAW A HOODED FIGURE

14.7.13

So, the trees are no longer decorated with strange southern fruits,
but Trayvon Martin still gets no justice when Zimmerman shoots.
The latter claimed he had the right to simply stand his ground,
but first, against police advice, he followed young Trayvon around.
Trying to decide, I guess, if the teenager really posed a threat.
But, judging by what Trayvon was packing,
he was as wrong as wrong can get.

He carried a sugar-coated rainbow that will never sweeten this pill
and a cold can of iced tea that he will never get to swill.
No drugs, no weapons, no alcohol, in fact nothing illegal.
So, what struck such fear into this man's heart?
What made him commit an act so evil?
Who gave him the right to challenge this young man,
might I enquire?
Why did he decide to start the exchange
which would end with fatal fire?

He saw a hooded figure,
who he could see was not his kin.
Yes, he saw a hooded figure,
but… he also saw his skin.
He saw a hooded figure;
he made his blood run red.
He saw a hooded figure
and the young man now is dead.

For forty-four days and nights
the gunman kept his liberty.
You can draw your own conclusions
as to just why that might be.
They claim Trayvon was armed
with the very ground on which he walked,
but he didn't bring it with him
and he was the one being stalked

by an armed man,
who chose to leave the safety of his car.
Why was Zimmerman not satisfied
to follow from afar?
I have a pack of questions,
but the answers are too few,
yet that the southern states lack justice
is surely nothing new.
For, while I hear the trees are no longer decorated
with strange hanging fruits,
a young black man still gets no justice
when it's a white man who shoots.

WE DIDN'T WANNA WATCH

We didn't want to watch, but this film,
this film cast the world as extras.
No speaking role for us,
just places on the sidewalk
from where we could not talk.
Simply the silent witnesses
to scenes that should not be seen.
I said,
simply the silent witnesses
to scenes that should not be,
seen?

But they were.

And now we,
we are all haunted
by the breathless last
of the life that passed beneath a knee.

Oh, to be clear, we are all sure this has happened before.
But this crime, we got to see... and this time...
the guilt just could not be any clearer,
and in that moment, we couldn't feel any nearer or any more
powerless.

And as the words of reason poured from round about us
we could tell that they fell on deaf ears...
and the darker amongst us, we saw our darkest fears.
Our ancestral mothers above us cried even more tears
for yet another soul they would see too soon.

But without doubt
what truly marked this out as a chalk-line for change
is how reason went unheard.
Those that were there had spoken the words
that we would have spoken if they had been us...
if we had had the chance to cuss

two bad words in his defence,
but in fact, we know, 'cos their actions show,
all the words in the world could have made no impact
on their indifference.

This is why fists everywhere have been raised in defiance,
yes, raised in the air past many a tear-streaked cheek
of those who now refuse to be so meek and mild.
Man, our anger is wild, and like your shame these words proclaim
there is a chance our anger may never be tamed.

But let me take a moment
to breathe.
Because that is one privilege
which I still have.

We've seen some try to shatter
Malcolm and Dr Martin's dreams
under jackboots
that wish to stomp
the green shoots
that grow from the grassroots
who know these three words to be true…

Black
Lives
Matter.

As to what happens next, well, that…
that is up to you.

ONLY CRIMINAL IF…

They say the Greeks have lost their marbles.
Well, now they want 'em back,
but it seems that looting is only criminal if
those looting are poor or black.
And, according to those who claim to be
not all that far right,
murder is only murder
if you ain't a cop that's white.

Yeah, they can kneel upon a jugular
and not offend their mates,
but to kneel sporting an afro
can cause heated debates
about respect for your country
that can't respect my kin.
Oh, it's the lan' of the free…
unless you have black skin.

So, how can property be safe
when the populace are not,
when a brother cannot run
without the fear of being shot
by those whose very job it is
to protect and watch their backs
against aggressors and the terrors
of white supremacists' attacks?

But how can they protect us
as they scope us in their sights?
How can they hope to serve us
as they disregard our rights?
The bricks and mortar are replaceable,
windows can be reglazed,
but no earthbound soul can redraw
the life that's been erased.

So I'm sorry for your losses,
but I just can't count their cost,
'cos I'm too busy writing eulogies
for all the loved ones we've lost.
They say the Greeks have lost their marbles;
well, now they want 'em back,
but it seems that looting's only criminal if
looters are poor or black.

IF YOU DON'T UNDERSTAND US

If you wonder why we're pissed,
then you surely must have missed
that Rashan's name was just the latest
on a very long list.

If you believe that we're too blinkered,
far too focused on the past,
note the keyword I just stated
was the 'latest', not the last.

If you think we're too bitter,
maybe you should taste time's pill,
a dose supposed to make life better,
and yet still our world's quite ill.

If you suggest the struggle's over,
clearly you are blessed or mad,
as I see lives that never have been easy
becoming ever more unfair and sad.

If you hope that we'll accept it,
that we'll just take it lying down,
well, I would watch your back
and hold on tightly to your crown.

As, if you don't understand us,
you might advise us to eat cake,
and, whilst that wouldn't be your worst,
it just might be your last mistake.

WHEN ASKED WHY

When asked why…? Why slavery? Why Tuskegee?
Why EDL, National Front or BNP?
Why Emmett Till, Stephen Lawrence or George Floyd?
Basically, when I'm asked, 'Why racism?'

I firstly have one word, and that word is 'exploitation'.
Exploitation which led to guilt.
Guilt which led to shame.
Shame which led to punishment…
punishment for the crime
of having the temerity
to survive just long enough
to be a briefly breathing reminder
of the shame-filled exploitation,
which, sadly, still breeds such fragility
that, it seems, for some,
will always be the awful reason
why.

SEED OF THE FRUIT

What if these once-shivering timbers could talk?
Tell tales about those who once walked between them.
The scenes they'd not so much seen
as absorbed with the salt of the spray
and the tears, shed in the triangular trade
in which so many souls were bought
and sold, young and old alike, back in the days
when the darker fruit of the tree of humanity
were just another commodity
to be transported for an unfeasibly large profit
on a disgracefully small fee.

A fruit which, like any other, could so easily spoil,
once it was separated from the roots and the soil
of the land where it had been grown...
from all that it had ever loved, all it had ever known.
Imprisoned as much by the high seas as the tall ships
from where shores were not visible for weeks at a time,
where hope disappeared beneath yards of sail and rope
dancing to the twin tunes of the whistle of the wind and the whip.

There are so many more than nine tales to be told,
including those of the weak, the sick and the unbreakably bold
who could not be cowed between stern and bow
and rebelled, somehow, despite the shackles.
Some argue those warriors, brothers, mothers and others
who never made the journey's end
were in fact the lucky ones,
but there were no winners here,
in the squalor between the decks;
for most, just unending fear and punishment
for the crime of not dying.

But that's a lie. For some, this gamble paid off royally,
building fortunes, cities, even empires...
including ours, those of Spain, Portugal and the Dutch,
all of which owed as much to the unutterably unholy sales
of not just the flesh present, but of the generations to come.
I wonder what my ancestors on board would have made of me,
seed of the fruit
of the seed of the fruit
of the seed of the fruit
of the seed of the fruit
of the tree of which they were the root.
Perhaps, one day, I'll ask them.
But until then, I'd ask you to remember them,
and to join the dots in the chain that links us all.

DIS PLACE

Some appear to fear most migrants
have carelessly misplaced their origins.
For what it's worth, they see it as a disgrace
that, for our sins, many here,
either by near ancestry or birth,
'ain't from this place'.
So, let us consider, transitorily,
what it truly means to be displaced.

People,
our populace is not like the waters
sitting in Archimedes' bath…
when one new body arrives,
we don't kick an old one out upon a different path.
And look, culturally,
these shores of yours whose virtues you'd extol,
well, they've always lacked an identity
that was entirely unified or whole.

Perhaps, given the intimate proximity
of these islands geographically,
the UK could be seen
as an aspirational template
for assimilation internationally.
From Picts to Celtic speakers,
via Roman and Viking intervention,
our anthems have clearly been
remixed with sounds from Angle through to Saxon.

And I'd say there's been
too many an influx or invasion for us not to mention
that even the notion of the nation of Britain was imported.
Yes, friends, that's right: it is a distinctly continental construction,
and one that's just so much more at home
upon the straighter roads of Rome.

And while all this history
from across oceans of time seems oh so ancient,
to this day attuned ears can hear
the twang of hordes of Norsemen in Geordie football cheers.
Our vernacular varies between sprawling cities
whose blurred borders have boundaries none can see,
and all our urban accents are deemed
to seamlessly incorporate voices from overseas.

So, whether those who'd advocate for UKIP
judge these facts arresting or not,
I'd contend this whole region has previous convictions
as a cultural melting pot.
It's a crucible which, in its last half-dozen decades,
has clearly come to be a little more black,
but if our pot's culture is diversity,
really, how can we consider this to be an attack?

Compared with all the Yankees, Aussies,
Canucks and Kiwis we've exported,
if some are feeling persecuted,
perhaps it's their world order that is distorted?
Let's not get into slave trading,
nor apartheid, in which Britons played their part;
there've been so many near-genocides
that I wouldn't even know where to start!

But then 'indigenous' is a decidedly disingenuous
concept when to our home it is applied,
since research shows those native to this region
to be little more than just an endless ebbing tide

with leadership that'd leave anti-EU monarchists
sent back to 1916 completely confused;
as King George waves to his cousin Wilhelm
across the bloodied Somme, they'd be bemused.

But if your wish was to avoid being ruled by Europe,
to ignore what's past is just so daft!
Because it's basically been that way since sixty-six,
when near Hastings Harry took one in the eye,
or since 55 BC when legionnaires first unfurled
bold banners beneath a grey-blue, British sky.

Look, people move! That's what they do;
it's what they've always done,
and from Austrian through Zulu
our empires are mere candle flickers to a sun
that's seen Homo sapiens spread virally
from an African cradle to reach from pole to pole.
And, once every inch between was taken,
from each other all too soon we stole.

So, when next some race hate monger
gets all up in your face and irate
about pure bloodlines, migrant crises,
Europe or our dwindling birth rate,
ask them to breathe and to take a moment to contemplate:
wasn't it always our diversity that made modern Britain great?

Introduce them to their history,
let them greet it face to face,
then ask them, 'Isn't it just your bigotry
we should be looking to displace?'

TWENTY TWELVE

When last could you be
this proud to be British?
When last did a Union Flag
strike so little fear into the hearts
of our darker-skinned citizens?
When could we see so many people
openly proud that we,
the immigrants (or their descendants)
nationally or even in this diverse city,
were on their side,
included in team GB?
When last could you be
this proud to be Jamaican?
Walking tall and harking back
with little or no fear of attack,
while even the police could smile,
imitating your countrymen's
style and swagger
with no reference
to guns, ganja or papers for immigration?

Where else are the things
people can do celebrated
above what they cannot?
How often does human endeavour
in so many forms
allow us to see perfection
in those whose bodies
are normally deemed imperfect?
Tainted as they undoubtedly are
by association with Boris and Coe,
by ticketing and security fiascos,
by greedy corporate arrangements
that seem to siphon profits
even as they silence prophets?
When I reflect upon this year,
I guess
I will be glad that they were here…
at least, that is, until
we come to pay the bill.

THE SCRATCHERS AND THE SCRAWLERS

We shall not forget
signs scrawled by Neanderthals
upon almost every wall we walked past.
An N, in form capital, with two lines added,
which digressed to suggest a capital F.
It was scratched into a table.
It was scratched into many a table.
It was scratched into too many a table,
often by near-illiterate authors
who wanted to blame others
for whatever ways they felt they
had been unable to express
their own oppression.

Hey, what better way, man,
than to oppress sisters and brothers
with more than a suntan,
whose fathers, mothers
or even more distant ancestors
came from another land?
I can understand why those who know
human history better than me
might see these 'brown beings'
as being from closer to
our only true
motherland.

So no, we shall not forget,
and when the next generation
of those scratchers and scrawlers
stands before us
with new letters and labels on their lapels,
we shall know them well,
as we have seen the proofs
that even when they hide behind the fake smiles
and the superficial dignity of a 'political party',
those who support the EDL, Britain First or the BNP

are just nasty, no-good little neo-Nazis
peddling the same ugly untruths
that were all too widely provided for us
by the inbred grunts of the National Front
since before 1970.

They will remain
deliberately unedited
whilst definitively discredited
and yet etched indelibly
into our collective memory.
So we shall not forget.

THE FRESHEST

Who's... fresh?

Were you born in London? I was.
But only because
my parents were moved from Brum and Lancashire
in order to end up here.
But arriving without the local patter when you natter
is a very bad idea.
Oh dear, oh dear.
As, if your voice don't fit,
you stand out a bit,
and may become known as... fresh.

Now, I don't mean as a summer's breeze,
blowing over a green and pleasant land,
or like a hot coffee pot
with the finest roast beans,
delivered to where you sit or stand
by the express movement of a waiter's hand.
No. This is a fresh on which people look down,
even those with skin so brown
that their elders would frown,
as they remembered what it was like to be truly... fresh.

Signs designed and displayed
to turn us away from homes and jobs,
in reverse: 'No blacks, no Irish, no dogs'.
Being sneered at and spat at by snobs, slobs and yobs
who saw not new arrivals
but simply newer rivals
for the few precious resources that they'd already got.
Rivals who might... work harder,
run faster,
not accept them as master.
Who, with tans and curls,
would teef all o' dere girls,
because our dance moves were slicker,

we moved our hips and rears quicker,
or, as dem say today – our moves were just sick, yeah!
You know what? Cha! I can almost overstand their fear!
So, in a vain attempt to try and suggest
that not knowing de runnings here
made us less than the best of the best,
they coined a phrase
which shoulda stick in dem crazy collective throat,
being so stuck in their ways
and way too lazy to ever see dem own dreams float.
Dem call us… fresh.

But the times move on;
the signs are now gone,
found only in dusty books,
colourless images at which no one looks.
Because they ain't… fresh!

And youngers here, well, they have forgotten
or just never been told
how our ancestors were bought and sold.
About Roots, history or even race riots,
there's so much for them to learn from our storytelling
griots.
About a mother who invited,
but contained people who incited
hatred of those they simply did not know,
in doing so letting their own intrinsic ignorance show.
They were not so… fresh!

But what saddens and amazes me
is when our bad 'uns use those phrases
to describe fathers and mothers,
sisters and brothers
who arrived after us.
So I wrote this short note
hoping you would see
it's mad for us to use this cuss,
as once it was not them but we

who were the freshest of the fresh off the boat.
This should not be used an insult nor a reason to gloat,
so raise your hands quick like Bolt, wave them bravely, don't pause to think
when I ask: would you prefer your neighbour to be... fresh?
Or would you rather they stink?

REPPIN FI DI LAN'

Reppin as I oughta
fi di lan' of wood an' water.
Credentials doubtlessly doubted by some
too ironwood green to remember
or ackee yellow to speak the truth
that unlike the Maori,
since our story was begun,
when you check back
we were never all black,
as out of many
came this one!

BOLT

When the man
from the land I love
briefly lets his cleats
kiss the track
between strides as he glides to gold
in the city I call home
the world will watch in wonder
in the knowledge
that in London
lightning did strike twice.

THE EMPOWERER

First his father gave him Rolihlahla,
'pulling the branch of a tree'
or the 'troublemaker'.
He certainly troubled some.

When he became a man
they gave him Dalibunga,
'convenor of dialogue'.
But he did more than speak.

To many he is Khulu or Tata,
the great one,
father or grandfather of a nation.
A living symbol of transformation and hope.

Madiba is his clan and is synonymous with his shirts.
It denotes from whom he is descended
when traced back two centuries.
He was clearly not the first of his line to be followed.

He is known to most as Nelson,
a name only received from his teacher
in a time when it was custom and convenience
to anglicise all Africans.

He has been called many things:
terrorist, Prisoner 46664, and even Mr President.
All justified, for he struck fear into the unjust.
And, while imprisoned or in power,
Mandela empowered us all.

JUST MAD ENOUGH

Some might have called him crazy,
for he said he could see the impossible.
Some might have called him meek,
because he would not raise his fist.
And some might have thought him gullible,
for he had faith unshakeable.

But let's apply the poet's twist to this.

If we lack the belief to stand for something,
we'll find we can fall for anything.
If we think arguments are only won by force,
we'll never see diplomacy run its course.
And if the people of vision lack sanity,
that means only the mad can dream.

I am so glad that Martin was a man
who was just mad enough.

THE DEFINITION OF PHENOMENAL

The definition of phenomenal,
with sparklers in more than her eyes.
Her body now laid down as merely mortal,
but still her words will rise.

A RAISED FIST

For a raised fist,
these two were dismissed
to spend a decade in the sporting wilderness.

Inspiring the minds
of those that followed behind them
not to be blind to their talents or the ties that bind them.

Upon the track,
not just the clock was attacked.
Instead, they showed the bigots they were proud to be black

An image timelessly framed,
set to a sour score of star-spangled refrains,
signalled their unity with all unjustly restrained.

Their brawn shaped by brains,
sculpted iconography that still mentally retrains,
because one fist alone cannot be raised
until first we break our chains.

POITIER

Hear me speak, like him, clearly:
we use the word 'legend' too lightly.
For this one, this one was so mighty,
burning a path defiantly with his ice-like dignity.

Few have changed so much mostly by being seen;
few have been so loved by the camera or on screen.
And none has seemed ready to carry his torch further or more
willingly,
nor did any walk this way before him so winningly.

Those who would follow him, we do so in awe.
As an artist he was all you could ask for and more.
As an activist he was measured, principled and true –
no need to ask if he was coming; I'd guess ya just knew.

Yet he got to live a long life,
and to die in the sun.
To bring the heat of the night
and see this stir-crazy world change some.

So send no lilies for his passing;
he wouldn't want us to feel too blue.
I just say goodbye to Sidney, with love.
P.S. We won't forget you.

JOHN BLANKE

As I look back across time
for the first in a long line
of black faces throughout history
to call these islands... home,
it seems to me I find the pages blank
(apart from a few Romans)
until I find the pages Blanke has filled.

Previous reams of white are barely broken
before these darker lines, too rarely spoken,
telling us no tales until quite lately
of quite how greatly Blanke was skilled.
So, while we know now what the man was paid,
we will never hear just how well he played.
Nor will we be sure if he could blow
like Davis, Satchmo or Marsalis,
but regardless, what we do know is this:
the tunes our Tudor rose of darkness played
included runs with climbs and falls
that scaled the very highest
of all our palace walls.
Despite the court being where it was written,
I contend one could be forgiven
for thinking his was a record
some still wish would remain unheard,
unlike the man himself,
who, with regal banners unfurled,
clearly trumpeted his own worth unto the world
as he weighed well his skills in earthly wealth.

Alas, eventually he slips
without lipped fanfare from our view,
but not before, both in and to
one of this land, this man was wed,
with his brown-skinned self not hid
by the violet gown gifted to him by the crown

(yes, he rocked a purple suit well,
well before many a famous prince did).

But seriously, I doubt 'John Blanke' was ever more
to him than a stage name: an ironic soubriquet,
something some deemed as funny.
Perhaps this assumed nom de plume
was found by Brits far easier to say
than the name first given to this
beloved Blackamoor, by his kith and kin.
Still, surely those insults would be surpassed
if at least by us that name was not made to last,
as to forget him would be a truly historic sin.
Blanke's story is a two-tone riddle,
which we see at best only half-drawn:
Britain's Blacke Tudor trumpet, caught in the middle,
but visibly of African ancestry born.

John Blanke Re-Imagined, by Ebun Culwin (2018).

*Acrylic, Gold Leaf on Parchment Based on John Blanke in The 1511
Westminster Tournament Roll from the College of Arms Collection.*

THE THEBAN LEGIONNAIRE

A name that is still world-renowned,
an enhaloed face in shadows drowned,
a tale, once heralded, too long concealed from view.

From Thebes to Rome then marched to Gaul
six thousand six hundred men, led in all
by a man who let his heart tell him what he could and could not do

Of innocents there'd be no human offering
to Rome's gods, its emperor or any earthly king,
regardless of the consequence this choice would clearly bring.

So, a martyr from a man of war,
a leader oft decorated was twice decimated,
as one in ten, once and again, were forced to pay the price.

Such dignity and instinctive discipline
was shown by a true leader and his men,
as all were forced into the greatest sacrifice, that

he was canonised, yes, made a saint,
immortalised in stone and paint.
You might have thought forever he had made his mark.

But later, his golden illustrations were taken down
for fear brown skin upheld could confuse folk in every town.
These scenes were quietly recast with players not quite so dark.

An Egyptian, a Roman and an early Christian too.
His story's entirety hasn't entirely
been given the respect that it is due,
as even his own church for centuries
chose to hide his skin's true hue.

So, eighteen centuries on, now only poets tell the tale
of these black saints
and their leader that from North Africa did hail;
in fact, many today doubt that this legend is even true.

But let's leave the fact-checking to those with fat cheques it befits,
hear hearts speak, not heads; instead
try to write for them an epitaph that knits
together the bravery of the Theban legion
in the legend that is Saint Moritz.

WHY DID I RETURN?

A posthumous poem in the voice of Walter Tull, 28.04.1888–25.03.1918

Until you've been under fire,
hunkered down in some funk hole,
you'll never know terror, the horror
or the damage to the soul
that just one barrage can do
before you ever hear the whistle's blast
that, sadly it's true
for all too many,
signals this'll be your last.

So some have asked me why I did it,
why I returned to the front.
Some have asked me why I did it;
was it just some newspaper stunt?
Some couldn't understand it.
Why would I choose to go back?
Some couldn't understand it,
partly because I was black.

But on many fields have I battled,
fought to win honour and respect,
demonstrated I was at least an equal
in matters physical… or of intellect.
While all the time being shot at
with whizzbangs of undodgeable abuse,
and always treading oh so carefully,
lest there were cultural land mines to defuse.

And in my darkest moments
leaders have shown me the way,
and in those darkest moments
as I've bowed my head to pray
I imagined one day I'd inspire
men to see beyond the melanin I inherited
to follow me, because they could see
my authority was merited.

So, no final cup hurrah for me,
no victory lap of Ibrox back in Blighty,
but I'd never swing the lead, you see,
so now I'm with the Lord almighty.
Amid the nightmare of the Somme
I saw some of my dreams come true
and, while you may be sad that I've moved on,
I hope these dreams inspire you.

MESSAGES ON… THE PANDEMIC AND BEING WELL

Since March 2020 here in London (and earlier or later elsewhere), the Covid-19 coronavirus pandemic has been an issue few could escape. Having been forced to self-isolate with the virus at the same time the UK went into a national lockdown, I found myself prompted to write a lot by what I called the Covid cattle prod: the constant jolts from never-ending awful news.

For those outside the UK, 'Five o'Clock' was the time that the UK's Tory government would broadcast a daily Covid briefing that was chillingly gripping and, quite quickly, utterly sickening.

'Borderless Language' is a snapshot of one of the better things that happened as a result of the pandemic. With so many people all over the world on lockdown, poetry events switched to online platforms. This meant that (sleep and time zones permitting) you could perform all over the world. Being pitifully monolingual, I was mainly involved in English-speaking events, from places like the USA and New Zealand (the amazing Your Place events hosted by RikTheMost are still ongoing). However, the event that inspired this poem was hosted in Malaysia, and the writing reflects that country's rich linguistic diversity.

'Crisis!' was a film commission by the UK homelessness charity Crisis for World Homelessness Day, to highlight the challenges that homeless people here faced at the end of the first major lockdown.

WHEN THE WORLD HAS STOPPED

When it seems your world has stopped,
it's hard to believe that for some... it is still spinning,
that some people are still gambling... and winning,
and so many are still more sinned against than sinning.

Clearly, this is not the revolution that many wanted to see,
but if you're lucky, you can still watch with me,
'cos the Earth's still turning,
its forests are still burning
('though happily perhaps more slowly)
and I'm still yearning for the learning that might come to be,

because it's still not still,
because we're still not still.
So, while we may stay the hell at home,
yes, even we restless will rest less

easily than before...
and you know what's more:
we'll also keep score
of who did what to whom

and why, and where,
and when these testing
questions which may not have survived
the neglect they've seen without us
come to be answered,

have no fear;
we will stand tall,
recall and tell all
who fortune allows
to live long enough to be there
what happened here.

I hope you're with me.
I hope you're still with me.
I hope you'll still be with me then.
But, sadly, so many won't be.

And these lines are dedicated to them
and to the many frontlines,
both the hidden... and heralded,
those that stepped up

and those who just kept up
what they always did
to keep us going
when it seemed
the world had stopped.

FIVE O'CLOCK

At five o'clock
the Tories dribble poison in my ears.
Trying hard to hide their perma-smirks,
they giggle at our fears,
trumpeting as triumphs
all the targets they've not met.
.They twist the truth like wicker man
and hope we'll all forget
that they failed to act in time
to protect our brave frontline
and they watched the death toll climb
while they told us we were fine.
But we weren't. And we're not.
And some of us won't ever be again.

But at five o'clock
they're back with another pack of lies.
Yes, at five, they just all talk numbers,
as yet another family cries
because their loved ones weren't protected
and our country wasn't led.
And so, to this indiscriminate killer,
our migrants and our working class are fed.

Seems our elders are expendable
as they're worth less than they cost,
but it's our dignity and our history
that along with them are lost.
They may remember victory in Europe
like it was just yesterday,
but when Boris was balancing his budget
that just didn't hold much sway.
Because like Kitchener before him
he only counts his flock by the head,
no understanding of the grief and suffering
of all those thousands dead.

For we are just factory fodder
who bleed to grease the wheels of industry, I've heard.
And to the Tories our cities are not peopled,
more filled with an ethnic urban herd.

And so again, at five o'clock,
the Tories dribble poison in my ears.
Trying hard to hide their perma-smirks,
they giggle at our fears,
trumpeting as triumphs
all the targets they've not met.
They twist the truth like wicker man
and hope we'll all forget
that they failed to act in time
to protect our brave frontline
and they watched the death toll climb
while they told us we were fine
But we weren't. And we're not.
And some of us won't ever be again.

LOCKDOWN

I wish I was stood now upon a stage,
with pews that were filled with a silent throng,
to speak in verse truths that might shape the age
or sing them so you all might sing along.

Remember when we used to share a space,
when words were close, not hidden behind glass?
Our passions were unified in one place,
blinding us to how quickly time could pass.

Friends, such times I'm sure we will see once more.
Your laughter and my heartbeat will be heard.
With clasped hands, souls will dance across the floor,
lockdown's bitterness distant and absurd.

So, baton down, and soon this tune might seem
a dim, discordant, unconducted dream.

BORDERLESS LANGUAGE

He sang in Tamil
while, perched on my bed's edge,
I ate pie and beans,
and I heard no words
but felt his hopes and dreams for others
transformed into visceral harmonic vibrations.
Then she sang
in Malay and Javanese,
flipping between
as easily and seamlessly
as I might shift my weight
from left to right.
And I thought...
I've fallen for this country,
these people
my eyes have never seen directly
in the garish brightness
of my afternoon
or the treacle sweetness
of their failing light.
And then... I cried in...
and shivered in,
and breathed in,
in a borderless language
we had all forgotten,
which, if it had to be named
(and I'm not quite sure it did),
I might call... human.

THE CORONA EXCUSE ME

This is the corona excuse me,
the dance of the polite,
where you weave to your left
while I dive to my right.
Eyes meet in a panic
as we try to second-guess
which path will allow us
on our journey to progress.

Perhaps, if one can pause,
the other can pass by
before we run out of space;
at least one of us must try.
But when one does decide to stop
the other does the same.
If we were to collide,
who would be to blame?

Impact looks unavoidable.
We're already too near.
We're clearly not breathing,
two bodies wracked with fear
by that which might pass between us,
by that which we might catch,
our ballet's choreographer
a viral load that might attach

microscopic barbs to our very being,
then work its way inside.
We wish we could have stayed at home,
but how long can we hide?
There're children that need feeding
and jobs that must be done,
fields and gardens that need seeding,
or hunger has already won.

So, strangers move at distance.
There are our loved ones we must not touch,
even though the anguish of separation
can sometimes seem too much.
And we'll dance the corona excuse me,
because we are polite,
until finally I slip to your left
as you swerve to your right.

CRISIS!

We will return – to work, to school.
To something that looks a bit more like normal.
Leaving the safe places where we have stayed.
Going back to games and the sports we've not played.

But for some, the lockdown was safer by far.
It meant not bedding down in the back of an old car.
For many, this return is something to fear
as the loneliness of homelessness in winter draws near.

The future's uncertain; that much all can see.
Too many can only dream of holding their own front door key.
Instead, surfing sofas, stuck in tents or huddled in doorways at night
leaves souls screaming; this just isn't right.

Because now, as we stand here, exhausted, pushed to the brink,
it's unacceptable some can only handwash in a public sink.
Homelessness has avoidable costs none of us can afford,
and these problems just won't go away if ignored.

We've seen what can be done when we work together.
We can find the space to offer everyone shelter.
Somewhere to recover, rebuild and stand tall
as we strive to find decent homes for all.

MIND THE GAPS

There are no happily-ever-afters,
just some gaps between the tears,
with houses packed unto their rafters
in which you can forget your many fears
surrounded by those who love you
and perhaps by those that you love too.

I do hope your gaps are many
and that your tears are singularly few,
for while our tears are two a penny
such gaps are quite priceless, it's true.
We can't know for certain how long each gap will last,
but regardless we all know this: they'll always go too fast.

BEFORE THE DAWN

I will gladly be your beacon,
or equally the hand you hold
in the moments just before
the dawn you fear will never come.

PURPOSE, HOPE AND LOVE

A sense you are important –
that there is more that you must do.
A sense things could get better,
although this sense may not be true.
A sense that you are cared about
and care for others too.
These are my essentials for happiness,
and my heartfelt wish for you.

ONE MINUTE

Just take one minute
to listen
to remember
to understand
to reset,
to step back
to refocus
to rewind
to regret.

Just take one minute
to rest
to rebalance
to breathe
to cry,
to think
to question
to reflect
to wonder why.

Just take one minute,
then, if you can,
take one minute more;
to work out what you need,
to decide just what this minute is for.

If you keep your eye on just this minute
then it shouldn't be your worst;
you might actually feel better in it,
if you can just
take a minute
first.

MY CLOSEST COMPANION

Sometimes, this fellow follows;
sometimes he leads my way.
At times my closest companion
can still seem quite far away.

I don't doubt he's a dapper dresser;
he's oft spotted sporting a hat,
though his figure frequently fluctuates
from tall and wiry down to small and fat.

He is easily seen by moonlight,
though his profile is lower at noon,
and I've known him to get completely lost
within one darkened room.

But I trust I'll always find him
towering once more at dawn,
while at my end he'll lie neatly beneath me again,
just as he did way back when I was newborn.

MY ABSENT COMRADE

A fickle and inconstant friend
of whom I rarely see enough.
It's within you my dreams reside,
but without you I feel rough.

You're absent when I need you most,
then sneak up on me, unexpected.
Can't you see you're broken and disjointed
when I need you to be connected?

But if we weren't to meet again
I doubt that I could I cope.
I fear it might drive me quite insane;
it's clear I'd lose all hope.

I doubt that I could heal myself
without your goodnight kiss.
Even the smallest dose of you
is something I might miss.

Since I've not fallen, I've learnt to accept
you're often shallow when I need you deep,
because I crave your company,
my absent comrade, sleep.

IN THE HALF-LIGHT

We were supposed to wake in half-light,
before the breaking of the dawn,
at the dying of nighttime and birthing of the morn.

Our eyes crave a moment of adjustment
in which to recalibrate
as subconscious cogs turn and internal switches flick
back to early from late.

We weren't designed to rise in darkness;
our sleep should not be disturbed by interrogating beams,
which return us to a bright-mare
from the soothing glow of dreams.

DANCE FOR DANCING'S SAKE!

As a kid, I did not dance,
but I couldn't tell you quite why.
It seemed that the very parental passion
that had brought me into existence
had somehow passed me by.

Perhaps I was a tad too sad,
or even too physically shy.
A gangly, bespectacled, curly-headed, goofy lad,
who far too rarely got to see his dad.

My mum, she tried to persuade me.
She showed me how to wiggle my hips.
But rhythm by me had been mislaid, you see,
unless I was flapping my lips.

It wasn't that it didn't hold my interest.
I even attended the very saddest dance class.
Their MJ impressions were far from the best or the baddest.
End result? I still wouldn't wiggle my arse!

Locking, popping and breaking were the top moves
by the time I moved up to big school,
but shaking my thang to beloved hip-hop grooves
left me aching and looking more foolish than cool.

Of the brown-skinned guys in my form,
at least half could spin on their head.
To windmill and caterpillar was considered the norm.
But me, I just was a non-dancing son of a dread.

Until I left my little South London 'hood
and found meself up in Geordie land,
where the dancing passed for good
was a strange and an arrhythmic brand.

Suddenly, I was the one with great rhythm.
All my moves looked remarkably smooth.
There were girls who wanted me to dance with 'em,
which did make my confidence start to improve.

Since then, no one could stop me;
I'd walk in and head straight for the floor.
For enthusiasm no one could top me,
though my spinning manoeuvres left me sweaty and sore.

I never did learn how to breakdance.
I still can't moonwalk or body-pop.
But I have learned to dance, man, for dancing's sake,
and vow now, while I can, not to stop.

YOUNG AND WRINKLY

You are not getting old,
but numerically you've advanced.
No, you're not getting old;
you're just chronologically enhanced.

You are not growing up,
but of this much I am sure:
to avoid growing up
we must become more immature.

We must dance until our joints creak
and sing until we can't speak,
laugh until our lungs ache
and love until our hearts break.

Yes, let's stay young together,
see young souls within our ever-paler eyes.
If we are to stay young forever,
we must become young and wrinkly and wise.

FINAL GOODBYES

We should say our final goodbyes early.
Early enough that their timing may be tinged
with fewer tears and with much more comic irony.
Early enough that any drip… drip… drip…
of slow and insufferable slippage
has ideally yet to even register.

We must find for them
the premature punctuality
that regularly delivers them ahead
of life's untimely surprises,
to ensure they claim their place
amongst the more dramatic moments
between which they will eventually lie hidden.

Perhaps, unknowingly, we already do this
each time we say *goodnight, goodbye,*
I'll see you, to the ones we love the most.

In these patterns of sound, so familiar
they almost pass unheard amongst the throng,
I hear the metronome that fixes our place
within the signature of our own life's time,
as the song of each of us fades or is dropped
in or out of the everlasting mix.

So then, with whatever suddenness
we one day find ourselves bereft,
we must take the time
to mine out all those moments
when we said just *goodbye,*
but really meant
I love you.

WHY WE SING

Because it is crippling,
something you can drown in for years.
In the blink of an eye
losing all sense of direction,
suddenly purposeless and heading nowhere.

Because it is a frozen burden
whose icy weight
both slows and numbs your soul
as it disassembles you into a pile of parts
that are so much less than whole.

Because it silences you,
physically robbing you of voice
as you are more than aurally swamped
by the deafening waves of life
that leave you bereft of the wind for words.

Because it strangles you;
a knuckled constriction on bruised windpipe,
vocal folds crushed until they no longer function
by the grip of tensions that prevent all vibration
beyond a rasping, rattling breathlessness.

Because grief can do all this, and more.
That's why we sing at funerals.

WITH YOU

You will see me
in your peripheral vision
from across a seething city street
as its waves of anonymous faces
swerve, blur and merge before you.

You will see me
glimpsed in random patterns
from summer's skyborne condensations
down to autumn's first fallen leaves
as each of these dances upon their seasonal breeze.

You will see me
stood or sat in places where I used to be
as if your love for me burnt so brightly
its echo has seared my silhouette softly
into your mind's eye.

You will see me
in a smile
seeming superimposed on a cousin or sibling;
in their walk, their shrug, their laughter,
you'll see mine.

You will see me
everywhere
as, although I will not be there,
at least within your memories
I'll always be
with you.

MESSAGES ON... POLICY, POLITICS AND PEOPLE

'Fair Game' was originally written to persuade people to join the Labour party and to take a more active role in politics in general. It has been repurposed to counter voter apathy at a local and national level.

'Is Anybody Listening?', like a number of these poems, was written as a response to the cuts to social security and local government budgets and the campaigns to oppose them, in particular that of Disabled People Against the Cuts (DPAC). It was turned into a meme shared widely on social media.

'Too Few Spoke Up' dealt with an incident within the White House briefings under Donald Trump, in which Jim Acosta was banned from the press briefing room.

'The Five Senses of Privilege' is a collection of micro-poems with the seven-five-seven syllable line structure, borrowed from the Japanese poetry form of haiku.

The section is brought to a conclusion by four poems that speak on the dangers of military conflict. It ends with 'A City of Many Bridges', a reaction to the series of terrorist attacks that took place on bridges of London.

FAIR GAME

Some claim they don't do politics,
'cos it's a game of dirty tricks
that powerful people try to fix.
I guess that much is true.

I too can see what's going wrong.
The same sad singers sing the same sad songs,
leaving no space for me and you
to feel that we belong.

But if that leaves us in a rage
that makes us choose not to engage,
we leave for them an empty stage
on which to tell tall tales
too short on other points of view.

So I beg you not to turn away.
Please know your value to the fray.
It'll be a dirtier game if you don't play,
but maybe slightly fairer if you do.

IS ANYBODY LISTENING?

Is anybody listening?
Is anybody there?
So many need support
and so few seem to care.

Can anybody help us,
shield us in our hour of need?
So many seem distracted
from our suffering by greed.

Will anybody speak up,
give our grievances voice?
So many sit in apathy,
forgetting it's a choice.

Will anybody miss us
when we're no longer here?
Too many lives are ending
now in misery and fear.

Will anybody share this
even if it makes them cry?
Too many battles will be lost
if we never even try.

Is anybody listening
to what needs to be said?
Too many pleas have been ignored;
they must be heard instead.

I'D BE A REVOLUTIONARY

I'd be a revolutionary
if I thought that we would win.
But losing is our lot, it seems;
it's just how it's always been.
I do not fear the name-calling –
Loony Lefty, Commie, Red –
but I do have an aversion
to being prematurely dead.

I know there are exceptions.
Fidel reached a ripe old age.
But if I tried to list them all
I doubt that I could fill the page
with names who flipped the status quo
but didn't pay the price,
and if so many made this world much better,
why is it still not nice?

So call me coward if you will,
and I won't call you a liar,
but this coward has dreams to fulfil:
dreams his death might not inspire!

MAKE A STAND

You can make a stand against wrongdoing
or stand for what is right.
Make a stand as a pacifist
because to stand is not to fight.
You can make a stand with a fist aloft
or stand with a lowered gaze.

You can make a stand that's popular
or stand without seeking praise.
You can make a stand by marching
or stand up by sitting down.
You can make a stand if your skin is pink,
yellow, black or brown.

You can make a stand quietly
or stand up loud and proud.
You can make a stand alone,
but it's harder to ignore those who stand with a crowd.
You can make a stand for others
or stand up for yourself.
Make a stand because to not stand
would be bad for someone's health.

You can make your stand on principle
or stand up for a friend.
Make a stand at the very start
or just before the end.
You can make a stand right now,
but if you do choose to wait,
please ensure you make your stand
before it is too late.

THE DEATH OF THE LIBERAL LEFT

The hoops jumped through by you are contortional,
but thanks to first past the post,
while your representation is far from proportional,
Brown's a prime-ministerial ghost.

Things may have stopped getting better.
They may even get a bit worse.
But your cardboard spine could not get any wetter
as you watched a dead rose leave in its Jaguar hearse.

Don't get me wrong, you didn't kill it;
Tony did that with Iraq.
The blood spilt here, you didn't spill it,
but thanks to you, the right-wing nightmare is back.

The first cut of the snatchers – was last night's EastEnders.
Such a shame that it won't be their last.
When they're taking good care of the brokers and lenders,
remember just how your X was cast.

You said, 'I could never vote Tory,
as I hate all that party stands for!'
'I'm a lefty,' well, was your story,
but I'm afraid you failed to keep score.

The yellow stain on your face, well, that's egg.
Your party's principles have taken a hammerin',
'cos, although you thought you were voting for Clegg,
in the end, it was you who elected Cameron.

WE HAVE TO

We have to cut the deficit.
We have to cut the deficit
We have to cut the deficit.

And so the cuts begin.
A race in vain for us to gain unsustainable growth
that half a million newly jobless know they surely cannot win.

But we have to cut the deficit.
We have to cut the deficit.
We have to cut the deficit.
We have to.

So why are the Tory benches filled with cheers
as all true liberals' fears are realised?
Surely this awful situation,
which apparently is all of Labour's making,
should bring forth painful cries and tears to mournful eyes
as it leaves the weakest and the poorest more at risk
and our vulnerable fringes even more marginalised.

Still, we have to cut the deficit.
We have to cut the deficit.
We have to cut the deficit.
We have to cut.

The mantra now is everywhere,
but who exactly put it there?
And really, tell me, do they care who's hurt?
I guess it's silly to suggest,
since this stems from overfed bankers' self-interest,
maybe it's them who should invest, to save us.
But no, in fact it's our welfare state that's to be bled,
our thin veil of civilisation which they choose instead,
far too quickly for us to maintain any modesty,
to divest.

As we have to cut the deficit.
We have to cut the deficit.
We have to cut the deficit.
We have to cut back.

Ever met an educated, homeless Tory?
Or one who thought their own rate of benefit was too high?
What has Cameron ever sacrificed to the greater glory,
other than a few fighter planes
that fewer still of us would ever choose to fly?

Yet we have to cut the deficit.
We have to cut the deficit.
We have to cut the deficit.
We have to cut back now!

Because if we wait too long,
a golden opportunity to reform will perhaps have gone.
So kick aside the needs of our union,
and sing Dame Thatcher's favourite song:

We haves just have to cut,
because we want to cut.
Forgetting those who have not cannot be wrong,

as we have to cut the deficit.
We have to cut the deficit.
We have to cut the deficit.
We have to cut back now!

Don't we?

TO REMAIN

Look, I like having legal rights – to be a citizen, not just a subject –
but I'm not without doubts about this great European project.
No, I don't fear drowning in seas of asylum seekers
some'd prefer out of my backyard,
but the far right's rise darkens my night skies
and I find some truths really are quite hard.
Yes, the status quo is twisted
so some not-so-nice people do too well off it,
but I fear if we leave now,
only the very nastiest of people really profit.

If I'm wrong I will happily sit and eat my hat,
though I know many a toff Tory won't be happy with that,
for they expect me to doff it, and tug me forelock…
but, bwoy, I'm two quarters yardie and one quarter Scot
and even the English bit ain't loyal to the crown
as it remembers all the serfs, peasants and rightless workers
these royalists have put down in the name of building a nation
of which we might all be rightly proud…
and so, when their anthems are played, only my silence is loud.

Peace trumps pounds, pomp and pageantry
even when it's been all dressed up in markets and sophistry.
'Cos I'm sure all those who fell in war must never be forgotten,
yet a century on, some would have us celebrate the Somme,
which shows those who know the history of the Tommy
something's surely rotten.
So, unless you favour all our disputes of thought
fought on the fields of Flanders again,
I would beg you all to vote, and to vote to remain.

TOO FEW SPOKE UP

When they came for the first reporter
too few spoke up,
perhaps because too few knew.
But then, even when the word had spread,
too few spoke up,
for they feared what he would do.
They feared for their positions
and the well-paid commissions
they'd lose if they were to speak true.
But history says they should fear more
the corrosive toll of silence on the soul, for...
that leaves scars time just won't undo.

UNLESS YOU HAD A CHOICE

Never apologise for what you did not intend,
for the line you could not remember,
nor for the money you did not have to lend.

Never apologise for the fact he hit you.
For the fact that even though you tried
you could not do what you so desperately wanted to.

Never say you are sorry
for the pain that I suffered at the hands of others,
even if those others were your brothers.

Never say sorry for the fact that life can be so unfair,
that innocents starve every day,
that injustice is everywhere.

To be clear, don't say sorry in sadness,
nor in anger, nor in fear; in fact,
never raise your voice in apology
unless you had clear course of action
and still chose not to act.

TO HELL WITH LOVE

Lord knows some say I'm a sinner,
and that that is true for most of us.
At this game, I'm no longer a beginner;
my lifetime has shown that I'm imperfect, trust.

But I have friends at whom some would quote the Bible,
suggesting their affection for each other is a sin.
To me those quotes seem distinctly unreliable,
as for me just finding your true love is a win.

And I know if my sentence for loving you
was an eternity spent below and not above,
well, I'd certainly take that – believe me, it's true –
as long as it meant I went to hell with love.

PRONOUNS

They may have been feeling uncomfortable
with him and her for a while now.
It is almost as though, now,
neither her nor he fit them quite right,
if they ever did.

But if that makes you uncomfortable with them,
could you explain how?
What is it about their pronouns announced
that upsets ya, kid?

Yeah, you might get it wrong sometimes.
I know I do; habits are hard to break.
All most would ask of you… is that you do keep trying
and offer warmth and sincerity
in all the apologies that you might have to make
while aiming to avoid your embarrassment
leaving others crying.

Why not allow humans to choose
which clothes and words each wears?
Don't claim that this small step
for you is just too tough.
Don't ask,
'Who cares if they prefer neither his nor hers but zir or theirs?'
'Cos I'll reply, well, them and I… and isn't them enough?

THE FIVE SENSES OF PRIVILEGE

Privilege – life's ice block.
The longer that you hold it,
the more numb you'll get.

Privilege is like
chilli. Those who've had too much
no longer taste it.

Privilege can be
like driving with headphones, 'cos
you listen but can't hear.

Privilege is blinding.
The more any of us has,
the less we see it.

If you can't feel it,
see, hear, or even taste it,
just sniff. Privilege stinks.

THE TOYS OF WAR

From the land of the wall-wishing brave
where braves are no longer welcome,
or this, our island of explorers
who now wish our sea shores
were fringed with endless rows of closed doors,
have migrated many mantras of woe
fired forth from the business of diplomatic show.

And so, below the same stars
beneath which some mothers starve
– but not ours –
some will still say we in the West
need to invest in joyless weapons
we claim we aim not to use,
so as to trigger in others
a will to choose
to use less useless weapons…
that, yes, all too often
we sold them.

We do this so as to terrorise the terrorists
until they fear us more than we fear them.
Hard, since we are so very scared
of all these very scarred
skins, minds and hearts,
because we know
history can clearly show
we marked them.

Yet even as we wend our way
along this well-worn path,
be sure, we will mark more,
and more, and more,
until we just can't keep score,
for so many bodies will have been lost
that no one can count the cost
as easily as the profits.

Still, we need be no prophet to see,
although with open arms some will cash in,
it is as true now as it ever has been before:
no progressive people can ever truly win
when we allow our boys to pay to play
with the murderous toys of war.

WE CHOOSE TO WEAR WHITE

Although many may have said,
'I think we should all wear red,'
my granddad, he knew wrong from right.

Sure, he'd remember all his friends
and their untimely ends,
and that's why he would have worn white.

As a prisoner of war
and a young man he saw
some sights which stopped him sleeping at night.

So, although he had 'won',
once he'd put down the gun
he was never the same, no, not quite.

See, he'd suffered since with sadness
and witnessed many madnesses,
all of which dimmed his life's light.

But at the same time
each immoral war crime
seen had clearly given him an insight

into what war games are for
and just how we keep score
and why the poor suffer more in times tight.

He'd be sure the state should care
for all in need and despair,
as charity can't cure the venom in their bite.

So he'd remember all their pain,
partly paid for others' gain,
and those too who bravely chose not to fight

in some conflict-swamped land
where men like him were forced to stand,
bowed beneath banners, far too bold and too bright,

designed to lead and to divide,
our rich humanity to hide,
when what's needed is to peacefully unite

behind a symbol less tainted
and less gaudily painted,
less bloody and simply more contrite.

And, friends, if after all that I've said
you still feel happier wearing red,
for him I'd ask one thing if I might.

Respect all remembrance,
respect survivors and descendants,
respect our choice when we choose to wear white.

REMEMBRANCE

Remember those who fell in war
and those bowed by scars
visible or unseen.

Remember those who were forced into uniform
and those who lost life or liberty not to put one on.
Remember the millions of civilians caught in crossfire.

Remember each was once a healthier,
more whole and a happier person,
a babe in arms so near perfect.

Remember them all
and heed the lessons that their remembrance must teach;
there are few threats in this world which
we should fear more than war.

WHO WILL WE CHOOSE TO BLAME?

Blame the poor for our economic troubles
and our unsafe borders.
Forget the one privileged percent,
the world's worst economic hoarders,
or the liars who took us into wars
we clearly could not afford.
Attacking terror overseas
has only spread its seeds toward us.

Sadly, too few seem to care
until they germinate in our backyard.
Some of us did try to warn you,
but your ears were far too hard.
It was all so obvious, not to be rude;
what else could you expect?

If fire and steel is what you exude,
that's what others will reflect.
We've made mad men feel righteous,
our actions drew their aim,
so, when cuts are made and blood is spilt,
who will we choose to blame?

A CITY OF MANY BRIDGES

In 'our land',
which retains its leafiness
despite how unseasonably
a fine few are fallen,
just beneath fury's fierce flame,
our city's many bridges,
a metaphor for so much more,
defiantly stand still.
Today I pray it's not just me
who hears them screaming silently,
'To join together is our fate.
We will not hate, we will not hate.'

MESSAGES ON... POETRY, WRITING AND VERSE

These poems are loosely about poetry, being a poet, or playing with poetic forms. Poems are pretty central to a chunk of my working life. I'm aware that poems about poetry are not everyone's cup of tea, as they are considered 'a bit meta' or too self-referential. But, when writing poems is a big part of what you do, references to poetry become a shorthand for generally being creative, speaking up or just feeling alive…

THE BIRTHING OF A BOOK

I may not be expecting my first son or daughter,
but like some old wives' tale I can feel it in my water:
a birth is just about to happen!
I have to scream to the whole nation,
lest they think I'm jesting about gestation,
a birth is just about to happen!

Overwhelmingly vexed by expectation,
counting similes instead of sheep packs no sedation when
a birth is just about to happen.
Bring me my pool, my gas and air,
send me best wishes from everywhere, because
a birth is just about to happen!

Printwife says, 'You're doing good,
just one more big push!' and whoosh!
At our new edition all will strain to get a look,
exclaiming in amazement, 'Wow!'
As it seems we are the proud parents now
of a beautiful bouncing baby book.

POETRY DAY

If this is a day
on a page or stage
that asks you to say…
something.
With rhyme or not.
Keeping time or…
stopping, to make your meaning clearer.
Bringing the distant nearer.
Unpacking the treasured memories
buried oh so slightly to the left in your chest.
Explaining why someone pushes all your buttons
(and how each and every button feels to be depressed),
and doing all this in words you feel
are more than deeply literal
or even a little surreal.
Yes, if this a day
on a page or stage
that asks you to say…
something,
then the question is
exactly what and how
will you choose to say
or write
right now?

DROWNING IN THE DROUGHT

At times I drip with poetry;
the words simply pour out of me,
a flow it seems no dam could ever stop.

Until I'm drowning in the drought,
a flood of salty-teared self-doubt
that withers, in the barn, my finest crop.

NOT YET

You're not a writer yet
if you still see your work
as merely just some poems.

If you're not a writer yet,
then don't forget
that you can just keep on going.

You're not a writer yet
just 'cos you 'might'
by the writing bug have been bitten.

And you're not a writer yet
if getting it right
still means more than getting it written.

WHERE POETRY IS FOUND

It's in those moments
that make us smile whilst crying
we find poetry.

It can be found as
the sun leaves behind a sky
made of candyfloss.

It can be found at
dawn, beneath the thundercloud
which could quench or drown.

It can be found in
the caress of a loved one
you won't see again.

It can be found by
those who still demand justice
with their voiceless eyes.

It can be found on
the way to tragedy
that makes you giggle.

It can be found when
time slows to a snail's pace, but
blink and it is gone.

It can be found if
you look in the right places
but don't search too hard.

Please do keep looking
for it, though, as it does seem
we can't get enough.

THE LAST MIC'S STAND

I bet you've heard a lot of great verses,
some well-rehearsed and others quite unplanned.
But what if that was the final mic,
and this was the last mic's stand?

Would we make a bold statement of silence?
Could all that pressure become just too much?
One last chance for minds to be opened.
One last heart or soul we could touch.

Would you choose to reflect on great beauty?
Perhaps attempt to right just one last wrong?
Tell a tale with fabulous oratory?
Sing along with a melodious song?

Which unheard voices would we amplify?
Which new lessons on this mic could we teach?
I guess I'd want it to go down swinging,
to test how far we can make this lead reach!

Could this cord bind the hands of oppression
and save those drowning in seas of despair?
Carry one line of hope to the lonely
and let the abandoned know we still care?

And if by some cable austerity
we then find that we've all just been mugged,
those among us with loud enough voices
should just continue with this mic unplugged!

You might think this is all too ambitious,
but I don't know where this mic's tale will stop.
'Though I doubt I can keep up long enough
to bear witness to that final mic drop.

I hope you hear many more great verses,
that you will write many more than you've planned.
Sharing them all before your final mic
is supported upon your last mic's stand.

IF BEING OBTUSE WAS AN ART FORM

He said, 'If being obtuse was an art form, it would be called poetry!'
Should I discuss dis cuss, or choose to dash into the dust,
far from us, like some kind of dutty discus in utter disgust?
'Cos poetry for me ain't about creating crossword clues,
nor showing off skills of syntax
by sending artefacts or smarty facts
by the literary equivalent of an illustratively alliterative, arty fax
whilst following a simple list of poetry's 'who's who's,
don'ts and dos.
It's about a poet expressing a part of who they are,
thereby allowing you and me an opportunity to see
from a cute angle
something that reveals to us a little more about...
we.

COPYRIGHT

Don't copy my copy, right?
If you have to copy me,
then copy that I write, not what I write.
And if you do have to copy that, then copy it right.
Copy how I think, not just where I left my ink.
Think for yourself instead of thinking as means of raising wealth,
as in the end it is only the thinking, not the inking, that counts.
Ink only serves to preserve so that others may observe
what was created when impulses crossed synapses
in that eureka moment between my many lapses
in which for sure I could have done so much more.
So don't copy my copy, right,
for the most sincere form of flattery that could ever be shown
would not be to imitate me,
would not be to imitate me,
would not be to copy me,
but for you to write copy of your own!

MY DEFINITION IN RHYME

I write rhyme
because I like rhyme.
I like rhyme
because sometimes rhyme rights me.
Sometimes, me, I fight rhymes.
Sometimes, rhyme fights for me.
But I never bite rhymes,
because I likes mine.
See, they mine my mind so deep
that even I don't know what they'll find.
If this was cranial surgery, my loved ones would weep,
fearing that my conscious life force must seep
out of my body until all that was left of me
was a shell consigned to nothing; well, except sleep.
But even if that was the risk I had to take,
from my lyrical path I could not break.
Please believe it would not be easy for me,
just the choice I had to make,
as now I understand, over time,
my rhyme has come to define
me.

PASSION TO COMPILE

You can't think without connecting concepts
or speak without synergising sounds.
You cannot write without linking
letters, verbs, adjectives and nouns.

To perform requires an audience.
Reflections are simply waves in thought or light.
You can only describe any one thing
based on sensory references coloured by personal insight.

So construct carefully your concepts,
synergise your sounds with style,
yet be aware even as we do this
we are but complex dot joiners, with a passion to compile.

SONG OF ARTISTRY

At times, I can be too busy chasing paper to pen much.
It's all too easy for creativity to become like distant family
with which, sadly, we fail to keep in touch.
I can let ideas just slip past me
like so many strangers in a city street,
and my old friend passion can become
a mere acquaintance with whom I too rarely meet.
But, so far, these flames still flicker, although they're oft buried deep;
our inner artist's roar still awaits a cue to awaken from this sleep.
Although we fear eventually atrophy may mean muscle memory might fail
that gears in our brain's machinery might actually seize, groan and cuss
due to the lack of strain or training (let's hope it hasn't happened yet),
with luck, perhaps our song of artistry might have lyrics that we can't forg

NOT THE MOST WORDS

Is it a block if I don't write with an incontinent flow?
What if my Ganges becomes a trickle
and there's a lickle less to show?
Is it volume that we should measure;
is life merely a manufacturing contest?
'Cos it's quality that I treasure,
not the most words but the best.

GREAT LISTENERS

Great listeners can become learned without ever having read.
Vicariously they acquire their libraries aurally instead.
For them the written word is but a token, so if it goes unsaid,
the thought that goes unspoken effectively is dead.

CHEAPER TO BANG

I got the invite via email – yes, out went the call,
'Come to Bang in Manchester, you'll have a ball!
We'll cover expenses – if the bill's not too tall.
Any profits on the night will be shared between all.'

Prices were cheap on my first look online,
but due to many uncertainties I took me time.
Virgin's twelve pounds each way had sounded great,
until I went to book and I found I was too late.

But when you travel oop north and money is tight,
you might not find the best price on a railway website.
Sure, they'll show you the quickest and priciest fare,
but caveat emptor – buyer beware!

There may in fact be a much cheaper way,
if you're not in a rush and enjoy the train's sway.
It's like tax avoidance – a bit of a fiddle.
You just buy a ticket to some place in the middle,

then another to ensure your journey's complete.
There's no need to lie, you'll still get a receipt,
but call it counterintuitive, daft or strange,
it might be the case that you don't have to change.

I warn, there isn't always a perfect connection,
and you could well be subject to dual ticket inspection.
However, I was still very surprised to find
the cheapest single can cost double the split fares combined.

So what if your journey's extended by an hour or two?
Yes, they'll charge you less to see more of the view!
That's why, though it's hard to believe, just trust me, it's true:
sometimes it's cheaper to Bang on a slow train through Crewe!

WE ARE THE POETS

You may not always have heard us,
but I suggest you sometimes saw us
in swift glimpses of clustered, uncool kids
finding their fun... in the thesaurus,
momentarily making our mental homes
in the very dustiest of the dusty tomes
or engaging in strange battles with self
that, once begun, could only be won
by building the best-spun of stunningly alliterative
and most assonant puns,
which were enriched by imagery so emotionally vivid
readers would feel it'd been physically etched into their eyelid
with a quill dipped deeply in the indelible ink
of every personal passion from the lascivious to the livid
in order to grip like the lichen of evidential proof
to the invaluable rock that is universal truth.

CURVEBALLS

Life throws us many curveballs
            from those that slip past,
tantalising, but simply out of reach,
            to each and every nasty body blow
                        that threatens life and limb.
            Hence, the worriers among us,
of which I am just one,
            can spend so much of our lives
                        trying to prepare
                                    for all that life might throw,
                        readying ourselves to duck,
            catch or protectively swing
something
            back into the future's dark abyss
                        of unknowingness,
            that, understandably,
                        we will all too often miss
                        some of the available amazement
                                    of this moment.
                        With our focus thus attuned
            to avoiding disaster,
                        we may also forget
                                    that sometimes,
                        although clearly for most
                                    not nearly often enough,
                        the balls of life will curve
                                    into a spot so sweet,
                        our effortless connection
            fires both us and them
        to places the likes of which
    we would rarely dare to see
within our dreams.

THE RYE CRIED

Before my eyes
deciduous trees on the Rye cried
tears of gently fluttering gold
to overpay our pavements.
It is a visible lament,
which tells of the seasons' insidious change,
setting a scene of late summer's end
and the start of early winter,
the passing of a year
marked in part
for both of us
by increasing rings
on
and within
our ever more wrinkled skins.

LIKE WATER

If I were wise I would know my own limitations,
but I am foolish enough to go beyond them.
I would desist when logic dictated I should,
not persist just because I could go on.
However,
like the water
that makes up
more than half
of what I am,
when I should shrink,
because the energy
which makes my particles resonate is dissipated,
against all the elementary laws of physics,
I expand to a volume which is greater than before.

MESSAGES ON...
LOVE AND FAMILY

Tributes to family, in the broadest sense of the word, and thoughts on all kinds of love.

SHE FED MY SOUL

She sent me out into the world,
but before she did, she made sure I had breakfasted.
She sent me out into the world,
but before she did, she filled my lunchbox.
She sent me out into the world,
but for my tea she prepared a banquet,

Gil and Benjamin broke my fast,
so, although I knew the revolution would not be televised,
I saw a poet could be hero in my mother's eyes.
My lyrical lunchbox overflowed
with the likes of Marvin and Shirley.
So, while things now ain't what they used to be,
that was no shock to me and my bridges are standing still.
My tea was rich with culture, politics and history.
I had no vast pocket money, instead an appreciation of each coin,
creating not the famished consumerist
acquisitional quest for cash;
instead, an insatiable appetite for equity
and an unquenchable thirst for change.

My diet was considered carefully
from my waking until I went to bed.
But, while my body never went hungry,
my soul was even better fed.

MY FATHERS' SON

When I quip with a sarcastic sense of wit
or search through near-endless analogy to find a perfect fit,
I am my fathers' son.

When I dance as though I own the floor
or select tunes to ensure others move even more,
I am my fathers' son.

I am my fathers' son.
This sentence may sound as clear as clear can be,
but, unless you can hear or see my use of apostrophe,
it's not quite such an obvious one.

I am my fathers' son
and, like them both, I am certainly far from dumb,
but, since I didn't pick them and they didn't pick me,
the cleverest one, I'm afraid, is surely none of us three.

If there's a credit to be paid,
and I feel there must be some,
my accompanying slip's account payee
should read, quite simply, 'Mum'.

THE GIRL WHO LOST HER SHADOW

He'd been a constant through some of the worst times
and gambolled his way through some of the best,
making her feel like a winner
in some of life's most important contests.
He was always pleased to see her
and so sad to see her go.
Their connection was near-telepathic;
whatever he wanted, she was sure to know.

He was quiet, protective,
ever playful and fun.
Sure, he was happy to walk
but delighted to swim, chase or run.
So he stayed longer than he was entitled
but, like all of us, he still had to leave,
waiting to make sure she was settled enough
to find the capacity needed to grieve.

For now, she's the girl who lost her shadow,
her heart's furry metronome.
The flip side to the coin that is her.
The being who made her house a home.
But she knows she was so lucky to have him,
and I was lucky she had him as well.
Will we ever be so lucky again?
Doubtful, but I guess only time will tell.

WE'RE GONNA MISS THAT CAT

Today Bella died
and, yes, both of us cried,
though we know so much is sadder than that.
Still, she was a good friend,
dignified till the end,
and now we're gonna miss that cat.

She'd warmed both our feet,
would be waiting to greet,
and before you could lay down your hat
you'd hear that great purr,
feel the rub of her fur.
Oh, how we're gonna miss that cat.

She was gentle of claw,
genteel and demure,
and we say this knowing it may be scoffed at:
we have known none better
and we'll never forget her
but, wow, we're gonna miss that cat.

LOOSE LIPS

She'd always loved to talk.
Now a few raspy,
constricted sentences can exhaust her.
But for me she will still try,
and, as I gently squeeze, the soft looseness
that covers what remains of once-strong hands
shifts between my firmer fingers
while, with a touch of simple wit,
I can usually elicit a throaty giggle
which would barely register as a tremor
if scaled beside the seismic belly laughs of old.

Still, beneath the thin white waves,
behind the cool, blue, cloud-filled skies,
between the folds of furrowed,
ill-fitting, semi-translucent human fabric,
sometimes, you catch a glimpse of her:
the mother of my mother.
A survivor of a bygone era
when loose lips sunk ships
and now a sad, old soul,
slipping slowly from this earth.

Two husbands may have preceded her,
but, despite an innings of ninety-three not out
and nine decades with nothing more serious than a cold,
she clearly feels aggrieved right now.
Perhaps it is the fact that her mother's tally
of ninety-nine years that nearly bridged three centuries,
weren't soiled by a single chapter of personal care
provided by persons paid for the privilege.
She says they are 'all so nice',
and swears it doesn't bother her even one bit
to have her bits cleaned by some young man
whose tanned skin, she says, reminds her of me.
I do believe her, but it's small comfort, as it seems

she's merely past caring about such minor indignities.
What hurts her most is not being heard,
even by those with the patience to listen long enough
for her misfiring synapses to first find,
then form her thoughts into sounds,
syllables and sentences.
This once-seamless process,
a dance completed with no awareness or effort,
is now a tortured limp between the mistakes
that mine her mind's field,
along pathways obscured by a fog of confusion,
where your partners' best-meant attempts
to lend a guiding hand
only point out how hard it now is
to stand on your own two feet.

Vocabulary has become an orchestra,
she an exhausted and short-sighted conductor,
desperate to play a familiar symphony,
but lacking the stamina even for the overture.
She knows the right notes are out there
and roughly where they ought to be,
but, batonless, she squints inwardly for her words,
faltering in the screaming silences their absence leaves.

Parkinson's is the wall she must clamber over
with every phrase now attempted,
each sentence a daunting assault course
separating her from being understood.
There were so few pleasures left,
so little she could do without support
even before this chat show curse of hers
arrived to attack what remained of her faculties,
and yet she remained sane
because even at her worst
she at least she could still converse
and she'd always loved to talk.

WHAT'S MISSING

When she was here,
she showed me how she mixed,
boiled and seasoned a list of ingredients,
which she insisted was far from fixed.
The herbs were key,
as was the stock,
but you could choose which peas
to add to the pot
as long as you had thyme and cooked them well.

Since she's been gone,
I have often tried
between onion tears
to ensure my beans do soften
before I add my rice.
But they are not hers.
They just can't be.
At best they're pale, bland facsimiles
of our 'Mummy's' famous rice and peas.

And, as I watch them cook,
I know no book nor spice rack
can help with what they lack
because what I'm really missing
is her love.

SHE WOULDN'T WANT YOUR TEARS

Twice removed by marriage,
her behaviour wouldn't show it.
Although we shared no blood,
we were family, I know it.

In the face of tragedy,
she was so humorous and stoic.
Some might think her ordinary,
but to me she was heroic.

Perhaps one of life's quieter ones.
At least, I never heard her shout.
But if you were loved by her
she left you in no doubt

that she would always be there.
All you had to do was call,
and she'd join you to party
or support you, should you fall.

She wouldn't want your tears now.
She'd urge you each to find your smile,
to remember all the good times
when she went that extra mile.

Her time here was such a good one,
which was so full of love,
and she shared it with a man
who fitted her, like a hand in glove.

Of course, we will still miss them both.
Their loss cuts like a knife.
But today let us remember her
and celebrate her life.

STEREO TYPE

Find yourself a spot
midway between the loudspeakers
to hear tell of the alchemic play
of an audio truth seeker
who, live or in recording,
weaves such a magic spell
sonic samples seem quite seamless,
such is her power to gel.
From a family of music
and with a dynasty to follow,
she's birthed bass tones so deep
in them a blue whale could wallow,
written random rhythms in time
with every soul's heartbeat
and made melodies that've given wings
to souls with leaden feet.
Supporting those around her
may not have made her rich,
but in providing positive vibrations
she has found a perfect pitch.
She's surprised many a technician
simply by not being a man,
yet her improvised soundscapes
have outperformed many a master's plan.
If you ever get to meet her,
sure, she'll play down all my hype,
but her life's scores leave me in awe,
or she's far more than a stereo type.

I CALLED HIM DADDI

I called him Daddi, like so many,
though he never fathered me.
He was 'just Daddi' to so many,
but first unto a very special three.

He was a great lover... of mischief,
a side he had not always shown,
but before his passing and our grief,
like his children, he too had grown.

Added more giggles to his wisdom,
emotions demonstrated to wit and charm.
Found fitness for life to be a religion,
which never did him any harm.

Remembering the ancestors
with many libations, mainly poured,
marked him as our great spiritual investor.
We banked on him leaving few listeners bored.

It seemed he always left with purpose,
and when he did, he often walked,
but he left no doubt he loved us,
and when I tried to elegise I balked

because he was one of life's great livers;
yes, he took its toxins out.
He was one of life's great givers
and all was easier when he was about.

His leaving was not so easy,
but it was mercifully swift,
and to one who lived life so stylishly
intact dignity is a priceless gift.

So yes, I'm proud I called him Daddi
although he never sired me,
for, like so many, I admired Daddi,
and Daddi still inspires me.

FOLLOW IN YOUR PADDLE STROKES

In this world, seemingly
so obsessed with sink or swim,
we must never forget the need
to simply keep your boat afloat.
Water can support a body
in near-perfect equilibrium
sandwiched between the states of matter.
But those raised between mates
that truly matter to each other
retain a confidence and security
that sustains them fully,
even when tossed from pillar to post
by the white waters
of life's most tumultuous seas.
If you take a canoe far enough
down almost any stream,
at some point, around the weirs,
the rapids and the rocks,
you will probably have to
come aground and walk,
sharing the load with those
who travel with you,
and, between the stumbles
and the small talk,
if you're really lucky,
you will build bonds
and memories
that nearly last a lifetime.

Balance and strength can be key
to any journey too,
propelled as you are
by muscle and sinew
which allow you to move upstream,
windward and against the tides,
because it isn't news

that the very best of views
are often not offered
by the easiest of rides.
But it is the ability to float
that sustains the fleet.
Life seldom offers dry dock
in which to make repairs.
All hands may be needed
from time to time to bail,
and while we will
try not to capsize,
we will not fear it,
for we know how
far we've come.
We know that support
lies fore and aft,
and as we cling
to our life's raft
we choose to follow
in the paddle strokes
of the ones we love.

1.0   <3

And look at you go,
Version 2.0,
an upgrade and that's no mistake.
I know we've both advanced,
we've progressed, we're enhanced,
but here's a EULA I will not break.
I'll watch the ports at your back,
guard against cyber-attack;
I swear by my serial key that's no fake!
Even with my mode set to stressed,
by my code, I'm impressed
by what high spec brother you make.

FROM YOUR BROTHERS

In a world of so few constants,
Jonathan is one…
which is why I'm proud he is my brother
although he's not my mother's son.

I've known him since we were much smaller,
but today I'd say he's still very much the same
as, while we did grow a bit taller,
he never changed how he played his game.

Always so calm and level-headed
as he plotted his designs,
and, as this man here is wedded,
I'm sure that all would find

that few of us are fairer…
but yes, my jest goes deeper than our skin
as my guess is, if you split him here and now,
you'd find fairness writ deep within,

because he knows about the struggle
and he knows that life's not fair.
He knows the meaning of good fortune
and he knows it's not something that all share.

And so he's become a man of some vision.
He's built some of his dreams, it's true.
But now, with both Leah and Maya at his side,
it's time to build some dreams for three, not two.

Yes, in a world of few constants
Jonathan is still one,
which is why he has so many brothers
who (biologically, at least) are not his mother's sons.

MY DADDY IS A RASTA

My daddy is a Rasta,
and he did what Rastas do:
tried to live his life with righteousness
and to his word be true.
But, one day, a blazing fire
began to burn inside his brain,
laying low this conquering lion,
who tried not to complain

when told that a blood clot
had reduced his cerebral flow
and that now how well he would recover
they didn't rightly know.
But one thing they were sure of:
he had to kick his one nasty habit,
that of smoking collie weed
with cigarette mixed in it.

You see, while the ganja was illegal,
the problem was the smokes. No jokes;
cannabis don't create the kind of fatty deposit
that chokes so many arteries
and makes airways positively inefficient,
although the fags are legally imported and supplied,
which is cognitively dissonant.

Doesn't it seem odd the deadly one's dealt legit
while the other is deemed illicit?
Well, as usual, growing at the root of many a wrong,
guess what, you'll find a profit.
It's true tobacco's bottom line
has lined all too many a pretty casket,
and we may need to dig up a very buried question
before we can begin to ask it,

which is…
if smoking is so bad for us,
why is it allowed?
How can it be justified?
Why are our politicians so cowed?

Is it that FOREST cash
buys the right to swing a deadly axe,
paid directly into sleazy parliamentary pockets
and, of course, in tax?

OK. So say,
without the revenue smokers raise,
our system has to change.
Well, maybe we could further reduce harm
by looking to arrange
fewer custodial sentences
for cannabis distribution,
since the hidden cost of a war on drugs
is the huge rise in detention

with the ugly social ripples and wealth transfer
that criminalisation brings
when people's wellbeing is valued
at less than the price of things
such as the stocks and shares
of prisonmongers like G4S,
or the wages of their fat cats
securely prowling around our markets
in £200 bowler hats.

Either both drugs should be legal
or both drugs should be banned.
Our system makes no sense;
it seems utterly unplanned.
But what's clear to me regardless
is change needs to come,
and if you can't see, here,
I speak the truth,
bredrin, it's you who must be dumb.

As my daddy is a Rasta,
and he did what Rastas do,
like him I try to live my life with righteousness
and to my words be true.
But he no longer smokes the poison
wrapped in paper, card and cellophane,
so that which once laid low a conquering lion
won't lay him low again.

BENEATH THE BRIDGE

To the family of Jim Smith, 11 January 1925 to 23 July 2012

Beneath Blackfriars Bridge are images,
pictures that show masons making magic
as stones, significant alone, were lifted
and then placed, one upon another,
held up by only a simple wooden structure
until they locked in tight to make the crossing.
If Jim was like those many humble timbers,
you are the stones built on his broad back.
He carried you until you found your place,
until you were strong enough to stand tall,
and through you, the curves of his support
and love will live on, long after his passing.
What a beautiful bridge you make,

which so justified his pride in you.

MESSAGES ON...
WORK AND PLAY

Since my work is often with young people and my play has often been music- or football-related, these poems relate to one or the other.

A couple of these pieces were written for poetry workshops, 'A Caterpillar's Tale' with students making the transition from primary to secondary school and 'Silly Billy' as part of an anti-bullying day for year sevens (aged eleven to twelve).

'Africa United' was written after I attended the World Cup quarter-final between Ghana and Uruguay in Johannesburg's soccer city in 2010. This remains the closest any African nation has come to fulfilling Pelé's prophecy that an African nation would win the World Cup… which was already ten years overdue.

A CATERPILLAR'S TALE

Today I am a caterpillar,
I am knobbly and green.
I cut that path through the leaf behind me;
it shows you where I've been.
I crawl slowly on my belly
and I am rubbery like jelly,
and if I should slip from this here cabbage,
I might end up somewhere smelly.

But soon I will go through changes
that you would not believe.
I'll say goodbye for a while to the cabbage patch;
a little home of me own I'll weave.
Then, when I'm closed up tight inside,
for few weeks at least I'll hide,
and only when I'm done transforming
will I pop back out with pride…

for I will be a butterfly,
soaring above the trees!
Yes, I will be a butterfly,
just floating on the breeze.
I will be a butterfly,
for it's what I'm meant to be.
I will be a butterfly;
it is my destiny.

You too will go through changes,
though they won't be the same as mine.
Yes, you too will go through changes,
but eventually you'll be fine.
As, when you do go through your changes,
you will not be alone,
and when you've done your changing,
you will be all grown.

I wonder what you'll look like.
I wonder what you'll see.
And when your transformation's done,
I wonder what you'll be.

SILLY BILLY

I am William, once known as Billy,
and back in my school days
I was known to be a bit silly,
although I never did mean to be mean.

I am William, AKA Billy,
and I was simply having a joke.
You know… just being a lad.
I never meant no one no harm.
I weren't trying to be bad.

You see,
I remember school as a place where I had fun.
Where my life got started, you know… where it all begun.
I guess while I was there I must've learnt something,
like in science where we studied the upthrust created by an aircraft's wing
or in English where we tried to explain just exactly why a caged bird sings
but if I'm honest, I forgot almost of all that.

'Cos mostly… I remember the people.
My enemies, my crushes and my mates!
The decent teachers we liked and the bossy ones we all loved to hate.
I remember we had a few arguments from time to time,
and no, we weren't all angels, but that's hardly a crime!
Some times, it's true, we got picked on by those above us
and I have to admit some kids, well, they got it worse than others,
because of their looks or their love of books,
their need to be neeky… to show us they were always right,
or the fact they were a bit geeky and the bigger kids knew they
couldn't fight.

But recently, I bumped into one of those guys online.
I think it was on Facebook; I accepted Jim's request, or Jim accepted mine
But we found our memories of school were simply not the same,
and I was shocked 'cos he said to me that I was partly to blame
for the fact that his school years were filled with tears and misery.
I said, 'Hold on, mate, you must be confused; how can that be?

It wasn't me who hit you, or dissed you, or even cussed your mum.
How can you be upset with me, bruv? That really is quite dumb!'

He replied, 'While I was being abused, you just silently watched.
You could've told them to ease off; instead you just sat and cotched
while those bullies made my life into a waking nightmare.
Bill, it got so bad, man, I couldn't cope. I wouldn't go nowhere.
I ended up housebound; I was too scared to ever go outside.
So in the end, yeah, I gave up; I just stayed home and cried.'

I remembered that Jim had got it bad, right up until year nine.
When we all thought he'd left, I said 'good for him!' and I hoped
                                                    that he'd be fine
away from all the teasing that he clearly didn't take too well.
I never knew, though, that his whole life had become a living hell.
'Billy, mate,' he said, 'you tried to laugh it off as all just one big joke.
But while all of you were laughing, something deep inside me broke.'

And that… was the last message Jim ever sent to me.
His profile just went quiet, there were no more posts to see.
I never knew how sad he felt when we were still at school,
but now I feel ashamed and, in fact, right now I feel a fool.

I am William, AKA Billy,
and I was simply having a joke.
You know, just being a lad.
I never meant no harm.
I weren't trying to be bad.

I'm William, known as Billy,
and in my school days, yeah, I was known to be silly,
but I really didn't mean to be mean.

HUMBUG

I only had one humbug and now I've got no teeth.
Of course, first, I ate the whole top layer of a chocolate box
and the one beneath,
but I only had one humbug and now I've got no teeth.

I might have eaten four slightly sickly sticky apples I won on the tombola,
drunk three extra-large and fizzy bottles of full-fat cherry cola,
had the whole top layer of the chocolate box and the one beneath.
But I only had one humbug and now I've got no teeth.

Perhaps the six marshmallow cornflake cakes were in fact a big mistake?
As were five finger fudge biscuits that I had just before break,
the four slightly sickly sticky apples won on the tombola,
the three extra-large and fizzy bottles of full-fat cherry cola,
the whole top layer of the chocolate box and the one beneath.
But I only had one humbug and now I've got no teeth.

It's true few could resist the eight party packs of sugar-coated sours,
nor seven super gobstoppers that each lasted seven hours.
Perhaps the six marshmallow cornflake cakes were a big mistake,
as were five finger fudge biscuits that I had just before break,
the four slightly sickly sticky apples won on the tombola,
the three extra-large and fizzy bottles of full-fat cherry cola,
the whole top layer of the chocolate box and the one beneath.
But I only had one humbug and now I've got no teeth.

OK, the ten months without flossing may have played a part,
and the nine years I forgot to brush were far from a good start
to those eight irresistible party packs of sugar-coated sours
or seven super gobstoppers that lasted seven hours,
the six marshmallow cornflake cakes that were a big mistake
and five finger fudge biscuits that I had just before break,
the four slightly sickly sticky apples won on the tombola,
the three extra-large and fizzy bottles of full-fat cherry cola,
the whole top layer of the chocolate box and the one beneath.
But I only had one humbug and now I've got no teeth.

AFRICA UNITED

Black stars in the dark that shone so bright,
pan-continental sparks were reignited;
in a floodlit calabash, man, what a sight!
Eleven Ghanaians became Africa United.

For the global diaspora of Africans
whose numbers stretched to billions,
a short but welcome distraction from conflict and debt.
From the highest to the lowest, military to civilians,
the togetherness observed there we won't soon forget.

Not a state of mass hysteria – it was collective sanity
in which differences were briefly cast aside by all.
Instead, connections rekindled to the cradle of humanity
by a team in red and a Jabulani ball.

Its conclusion could have been seen as a downright tragedy,
but something bigger than a penalty would be missed
if the result on the pitch, which was an obvious travesty,
obscured the euphoric unity by all witnessed.

It was here, we felt it. In spite of the result,
this game of beauty reminded us that whilst life is still unfair,
as we journey through it from childhood to adult,
it's less about the winning than the experience we share.

Black stars in the dark that shone so bright,
pan-continental sparks were reignited;
in a floodlit calabash, man, what a sight!
Eleven Ghanaians became Africa United.

THE BANSHEE IN ROW D

An unscreamed message to the lino
from me, the bloke in the fourth row.
What happened here, perhaps you missed it,
though quite how... I'll never know.

For that forward was offside
even before he took a dive,
though after all the rolling and the screaming
it is a shock he's still alive!

Now, I know the move was slick;
they countered quickly on the break.
But, my dear friend in the black,
you were miles behind the play, for goodness' sake!

Did you stumble, take a tumble,
drop that flag you've been so keen to wave?
And only look back up in time
to see our keeper make the save?

Was what had just transpired simply
a mystery at which you could only guess?
Was it an attempt to save your blushes
that resulted in this officiating mess?

Now, I know you wouldn't cheat us
(well, at least not with intent).
I'm trying hard not to be holier-than-thou,
but that decision wasn't heaven-sent,

'cos we conceded that penalty
and went on to lose the match.
Our fortress breached with soiled sheets,
defeat on our home patch.

And so, I pen to you this missive,
in the hope you might reflect.
Signed, the banshee in row D of block fourteen
with, I hope, a modicum of respect.

FOOTBALL'S PROBLEM

We've heard sectarian and racist hate,
seen a governing body in a sad old state,
fans forced to flee flying fists in fear,
but football's problem is not just beer.

We've neo-Nazis, ultras and yobs,
most of whom must hold decent jobs.
Some come just for the fight, I hear,
so how can football's problem be just beer?

We overpay schoolboy primadonnas
to create cheap imitation Maradonas
for a sinister business class in the middle tier
who know football's problem is not just beer.

It's all awash with funny money
that rains from the sky on days quite sunny.
Oligarchs don't just pay to make us cheer,
so football's problem can't be just beer.

Some peacefully drink, and sing and dance
their way through every night in France.
So, please, can we be completely clear:
football's problem is not just beer.

ORANGES

Cold, crisp, early Sunday morning,
a personal fog cloud forming
after waiting, boot bag in hand,
for a lift or a bus
to some far-flung field

to eye an opposition
all too often filled with giants
who we would try to beat
with pace and power,
trickery and heart,

but most of all with teamwork
and with partnerships in which
the collaborative units
were of far more value
than the sum of all their parts.

I guess we shared more than oranges
as together, on and off the pitch,
we exhausted our bodies
but revitalised our souls
to kick off and go again.

NETS OF BRICK

Sure, we've scored in nets of brick and mortar,
slid in on turf that was more like concrete.
Played on pitches with half-marked boundaries,
shins bare, no studs to stabilise our feet.

No replays to assist our decisions
(except perhaps those playing in our heads),
and yet somehow the games kept on going,
bibs v. skins, or uneven blues v. reds.

'Cos it was the ball that brought us together,
more than the dreams of ever lifting the cup.
Chasing thirty-two panels of leather,
we learnt mutual respect and grew up.

WE SPOKE FOOTBALL

My friends came from all over the place
while I barely had to dribble round the corner,
but we all found ourselves kicking a ball
in the same local park.

English was a second language
'cos here we spoke football, first, last
and in between: a vocabulary so familiar,
however far the journey to this point had been.

And we knew these slopes and the uneven ground,
the sticky patches where the ball could never bounce.
We all had dreams of victory on these muddy fields,
but, just by being here, some amongst us had already won.

NO MORE CHOICE

It started at 100 with a Kiss
and then, at the dial's heart, another,
with a hissier signal that was easier to miss.
Suddenly those in London who loved a black voice
started to get spoilt by the concept that was Choice!
Those previously at the mercy of the DTI
were now legal broadcasters to you and I.
It was such a unique and exciting time for us as a group,
my spars and I listened to the test broadcast on a continuous loop,
and then, when I went to the regions,
I dissed stations like Galaxy
who flipped the script continuously
to squeeze in pop tracks to a playlist
apparently compiled haphazardly,
as in London we listened differently.

Back then our stars controlled the mic, they were front and centre,
not sidelined to some afterthought lazily labelled Xtra.
But those days are now gone. Long-lost rare grooves,
they fade fast as the wallpaper in some shoobs blues.
Seems those who mek we dreams come true
were more up inna de business of business than of music…
and so it became less about singers and bands
and more about selling us brands,
and eventually it seems our very soul was sold.
So ever so slowly, once more, London's airwaves
became a sea of dancey, unabashedly bashmentless raves
whose melodic flesh was plucked clean by the corporate vulture
hungry for hooks and B-lines more often seen in roots and culture.

Still, this is only the latest movement
to pass in our bass-driven symphony.
It cannot and must not be the last; we can get an encore, surely?
So fire up the RSL transmitters, go online or turn to DAB;
in fact, like old Queen Bess, I will even condone piracy

to ensure we do not forget
and are not once more wiped from history.
Surely we must yet again
take control of our electromagnetic legacy.

PUNK POETRY

When rebellion was conformity
and Mohicans were the norm.
When Never Mind the Bollocks
took the UK charts by storm.
When the NF thought they had the right
to march on London's streets.
When lovers and punk were the greatest rocks
and the latest dancefloor beats.
When many dreadlocks were still forming
and safety pins started adorning
some places people thought
no pin could ever safely go.
One bunch of social BS detectors,
audio unrest and injustice reflectors
crept loudly from suburban garage land
and, with a new brand of punk poetry,
stole the show!

THE KEEPERS' VIEW

When you first passed through them,
all butterflies and sparkling eyes,
bouncing bundles of boundless potential
in sharp creases and glistening shoes,
you will barely have noticed the silent sentries
marking the boundary between your worlds
of heavenly refuge and interminable imprisonment.

Back and forth for years, growing as you go
like a tide, each droplet herded ever onward
by buzzers and bells to meet your future selves.
You will inscribe a path across this margin.
So focused on the now, all change is imperceptible.

Until, perhaps, a brief moment of reflection,
which often strikes only as you walk out
and they close behind you for the final time.

We need to weave the silvery strands
of poetry that line life's thunderclouds
into a canopy to cover all humanity.
For I fear the storm that I see coming,
and that we may not have seen
the worst of it quite yet.

The devil may be in the detail,
but that's also where the divine resides.

ACKNOWLEDGEMENTS

To the many friends and family who helped to inspire many of these poems; I hope many of you can find yourselves in these pages. This book couldn't exist without your inspiration, love and support.

To everyone at Burning Eye, thanks for the opportunity to get this out into the world and to both Harriet Evans and Bridget Hart for your patience with all the practicalities.

To the small(er) group of poetic friends who have lifted me, listened while I agonised over lines, words and the poems that never made the cut... in particular, Kat Francois, Steve Tasane, Fay Roberts, Naomi Woddis, and Rikki Livermore... but this list gets embarrassingly long very quickly, so if you're not named please know you're not forgotten.

To Sarah the muse with whom I share my world, and my mum without whom I wouldn't be; thank you.